To my twin sons and daughter, all of whom participated in the Student Christian Movement. Each of them has enriched my life; Ralph and Mary Jean here, Bob both here and already from beyond.

The Student at Prayer

Compiled by

H. D. BOLLINGER

THE UPPER ROOM
Nashville, Tennessee

UR-129-15-0860
Printed in the United States of America

FOREWORD

This is a very simple book of prayers. It is hoped that it may be helpful to college and university students.

The writers of the prayers are students, directors of student work, pastors, faculty, administrators, and leaders in the Student Christian Movement around the world. To each we are grateful for his contribution.

It has been a pleasure to compile these prayers. The response has been generous, kindly, and personal.

—H. D. BOLLINGER

CONTENTS

7

8

PRAYER

Prayer is finding oneself in proper relation to almighty God. It is the process of becoming adjusted to the will and purpose of God. It is much more than conversation with God. It is *the involvement of one's whole self with God.*

To Whom Do We Pray?

Primary to this relationship is to know who God is. If we enter into conversation with Him, we must in some way know Him. If we pray to God, we must have an image in our mind of what He is like.

Sometimes people have strange ideas of God. For many He is a parent image. For others He is like a grandfather. For still other people He is like Santa Claus. In fact, one contemporary artist pictured God coming out of a storm with his whiskers flowing.

How does one think of God when one prays? Some persons close their eyes and try to sense an atmosphere of God, a sort of all-pervasive spiritual presence. This is not bad, but is it the full Christian sense in which the Christian should image God when he prays?

Our Heavenly Father

The Christian, different from a person of any other religion, is very fortunate in his image of God because *God is like Christ.* Therefore, as the Christian prays he comes to God in Christ. He visualizes the Master and prays to God in the name and for the sake of Jesus Christ. God has been manifested to the Christian on this earth and in history; and God, therefore, to him has become very real and very personal. As the Christian senses how God acts in history through Jesus Christ, he comes to know God in person and as a presence. Prayer then becomes natural, real, and personal.

Prayer is fellowship and communion with God. It is getting in touch with the Eternal. It is having fellowship with the Creator. It is *being* expressing relationship with *Being.* It is getting out of oneself and into harmony with the Divine. It is the finite creature coming to the Infinite. What does all this mean? Let us begin with ourselves. We are

9

creatures of the earth, limited in time and space. God has made us what we are—"in the image of God" and "a little lower than the angels." Since we are creatures of the flesh and children of the earth, does it not seem queer that we should even *think* we could get in touch with God, let alone have fellowship with Him? No, it is not queer! We are sons and daughters of the living God. We are His children; and children have a right to have communion with their parent, Father, God.

Prayer, then, is communion and fellowship with God. It means entering into proper relationship with our heavenly Father. It means we are never alone but always have companionship with God. It means that where He is we can be also. It means that His infinite power is available to us in all places and under all circumstances.

Alone—or with God

One can never know what this communion with God really means until one feels left alone. This is the most terrible experience of all life—to feel deserted. To be alone and thus lack fellowship is like hell itself. Conversely, the exact opposite is true. To be with God and have fellowship with Him is like heaven. To know that the God of the universe really cares is the most comforting thought man can experience. Prayer is having this fellowship.

What does fellowship with God mean? From the human standpoint, it means that one can be lifted into the presence of God. This is an experience like no other in all human existence. *It means moving from the small island of selfhood into the vast outreaches of otherness where God dwells.* It means one can be himself and more because through prayer he becomes more than himself through fellowship with God. The uplift and outreach that this gives to an ordinary person is unlimited.

From God's standpoint, His fellowship with man seems to mean something, also. Now, no one can ever know the mind of God. However, the picture of God that the Christian gets all through the New Testament is of a loving heavenly Father who loves and cares for His own. He seeks and searches for the last, the least, and the lost. If God is like Christ, He cares for His prodigals; He cares for the

10

sparrows that fall and for His close friends who betray Him. In fact, it must be that *when man prays, God's heart is moved to respond in fellowship with man,* howsoever great a sinner he may be.

There is a position in psychology concerning the self that is very important in understanding prayer. It is the idea of acceptance. It is a state of understanding oneself wherein a person *accepts* himself for what he really is. For example, each self is composed of many selves. We are one self to the family; another self in the university; and many times another self to ourselves. In fact, most of us are always trying to be a self other than our real self. Sometimes we cannot pray because we ourselves rebel at the idea of being what we *really* are. Now, in prayer there is the opportunity to be the real self that we actually are. Pride many times keeps a man from accepting his real self. In prayer, a man had better come to accept his real self, for what else can God accept but ourselves. Acceptance, then, in prayer means offering our real self to God. It requires self acceptance first, then offering.

However, there is more to this self-acceptance business than meets the eye, especially in prayer. When a man offers his real self to God in prayer, it means giving to God all that he is and has. All that he is? Yes. Does this not mean he banishes his pride? Yes. And confesses his sins to God in prayer? Yes, yes. These are the necessary steps in prayer. *A person can never have real power in prayer unless he lays his life out before God just as it is.* Anything secret, hidden, or held back from God hinders communication.

Some may argue that since God knows our thoughts and how we act, "Why bother to tell Him about it?" The answer is that He has made us psychologically and spiritually in such a way that fellowship with Him comes only when the channels of the soul are cleared for it. Confession then becomes one of the most important aspects of prayer. The entire burden of the soul's guilt must be confessed before almighty God. Pride, lust, envy, selfishness, deceit, and sin in any form must be brought to light and laid bare.

When a person becomes honest with God, there is a new integrity of relationship that becomes established. It is a meager observation to

11

say that God is honest, but nevertheless *the moral nature of the universe seems to sustain goodness* when it comes clean in confession. New power, new hope, new life come into the sinner's soul when in prayer before God he sees and accepts himself as he really is. This is because God accepts him, also.

The Meaning of Confession

What does it mean to confess one's sins to God? At the outset, it means absolute honesty. It is utterly impossible to hide anything from God. An attempt to do so is self-delusion. Furthermore, it is dishonest. It is tempting the nature of things. It has in it the element of futility, of hopelessness. It is entirely possible, of course, that one would hesitate to confess his sins before some people. In fact, this is the danger of the confessional, namely, that many times one confesses his wrongdoing before a person who is not prepared to receive such information. This is not true of God, and *the freedom that one can have in prayer is in knowing that God almighty can receive our outburst of confession and guilt.*

Changing Relationships

This brings us to the observation that there is something almost terrifying about prayer, that is, *if it is real prayer. Prayer is the business of changing relationships.* Prayer lifts a person out of himself and what he is into a better condition and experience. Prayer strips a person of sham, self-conceit, and bravado and places him before God in penitence and humility. It cleanses and clarifies. Prayer enables a man to be in touch with the ultimate power of the universe, the power of God. Prayer is laying hold of the moral nature of the universe. It is coming to grips with the ultimate. This would be terrible were it not for the fact that the power comes from a loving heavenly Father.

When a person confesses his guilt to God in prayer, God is quick to forgive his sins. The outpouring grace and goodness of God is one of the deep mysteries of the spiritual realm. Forgiveness takes place when a broken and contrite heart opens to the reservoirs of God's love. It is perhaps here in prayer we are in greatest need of our formulas of faith. How can we know our sins are forgiven? How can we experience this vast outpouring of God's love and grace?

12

In response to these questions, let us remind ourselves of the image of God in Christ Jesus. God was in Christ reconciling the world unto Himself. Thus Christ gathered unto Himself a group of disciples, men like ourselves, who sought to be His companions in the trials and tribulations of ordinary life. God's plan of salvation called for the proclamation of the gospel, the good news in Christ. This gospel was rejected in His age, and even His disciple friends were faithless and unbelieving. The Christ was taken to a cross; and after His death, in some manner, He came again as the risen, victorious Christ. This drama brings before us in panorama rejection first and then resurrection. It is the story of sin and salvation. *Just as surely as in the world there is sin, rejection, and suffering, so likewise there is forgiveness, acceptance, and victory.* Jesus in history, then, proclaims to the Christian that there is no sin, however dire and evil it may be, but that there is also salvation and forgiveness and love. The sinner as he prays confesses his sins in faith, knowing that God forgives.

To add to the reality of forgiveness is to experience it. A lost relationship with God is a dreadful, lonely experience. A restored relationship is a blessed, happy one. That is why so much prayer to God should be filled with gratitude, thanksgiving, praise and joy. *There is nothing in all the world to compare with a full, free, and happy relationship with almighty God.*

Estrangement and Reconciliation

We all have experienced in some way estrangement from our fellow man. For example, we like our friends and loved ones; but somehow, in the day's work, tensions and misunderstandings arise. Communication is difficult, and we wonder how things can be made right. Finally, reconciliation takes place and there is the restored relationship. These minor tensions and restored relationships of us humans are nothing as compared to the glory and gladness of prayer when one realizes that the channels to the infinite are cleared and we are again in happy fellowship with God. This kind of release and restoration should take place every time we pray. Our world, our culture, and our times are so cluttered and clogged with hindrances to fellowship with God that *each day this fellowship must be renewed and restored.*

13

We might as well admit that we do not fully know how to pray. The disciples did not know how and requested of Jesus, "Master, teach us to pray." There is something about prayer that makes it a difficult experience. It is the spirit of man speaking with the spirit of God; and where things of the spirit are involved, most of us are inexperienced. Because of this fact, to lead the life of prayer requires discipline, learning; in fact, hard work. What helps should one have available to learn to pray?

The Curriculum of Prayer

At the outset, one should establish the circumstances and curriculum of prayer. When a student enrolls in a course, he enters into a certain discipline of behavior in order to read, study, absorb, and experience the subject at hand. This is even far more true in prayer. *A specific time and place for prayer should be set,* and the individual student should hold to this rigidly—far more rigidly than any subject he will ever take in college. It should always be kept in mind that life-changing experiences are involved in prayer.

Things in Order

The person who prays should also set in order, insofar as possible, his total religious experience. Specifically at this point we have in mind theology, which is an ordered statement of faith. Thus a Christian person should clarify, insofar as possible, what he thinks and believes about the great ideas, tenets, and principles of the Christian faith. When a person is just beginning the life of prayer, it is important that he clarify what he thinks about God, Jesus Christ, the Holy Spirit, sin, salvation, the nature of the gospel, the kingdom of God—in fact, all the main essentials of the Christian faith. *In these days there is no excuse for a Christian being foggy or unclear in his beliefs.*

Religious Growth

In prayer which is one's total life adjustment to God, a person should grow in religious experience. There is nothing wrong in being a freshman in college, but there is something terribly wrong in being a freshman for four years. In fact, one of the thrills of an education is for a person to experience new horizons of intelligence. In a far more

14

significant manner, this is true in the life af prayer—for one to gain new perspectives, insights, and understandings of faith. Therefore, the praying person should consciously *"stake out"* *expansions of faith to be gained and developed in days ahead.*

The Discipline of Prayer

Prayer that is genuine requires discipline. This is true not only of prayer but also of anything worthwhile. The athlete trains long hard hours that in the moment of contest he may acquit himself in the best possible manner. Thus we recommend that a praying person: (a) Read the literature of prayer, (b) utilize the poetry of prayer, (c) develop a vocabulary of prayer, (d) practice a regular discipline of prayer.

There are two ways of praying, alone and with others. The Bible records many experiences of both, and both are necessary. To pray only in the presence of others invites hypocrisy. Therefore, there should be *established a habit of private prayer,* regular and a part of oneself, like eating. It is well, also, to become a member of a prayer fellowship, for one can grow in prayer by praying with others. Furthermore, when two or three are gathered together in the name of God and in the spirit of prayer, there the Lord will be present.

Prayer Can Be Selfish

Prayer is always in danger of becoming selfish. Since it is a clarifying, comforting experience, the tendency is to repeat its satisfactions just because they satisfy. It is also true that prayer can be very much misunderstood. There is a certain very quiet calmness or peace of mind that can be obtained in prayer that is exceedingly selfish. In fact, it can encourage the kind of ingrown religious experience that makes good people, we regret to say, "good for nothing." Here then is the heart of prayer, and, we believe, the heart of the Christian faith. *Prayer, being a religious experience, must always go beyond itself.* Prayer becomes hollow mockery when one prays for self and loved ones only, but prayer changes things when it is linked to Christian action.

Prayer and Action

It can never be emphasized too strongly that prayer is making a total life adjustment to the will and purpose of God. *Prayer, then, properly understood, involves the whole being in all relationships.* To put it plainly, he who prays is concerned with the health and welfare of all mankind; and he acts accordingly. Our world is full of hate, injustice, disorder, mistrust, and ill will. *It requires the concerned action of Christians to bring peace and justice and harmony into the social order.* Just the words and ordinary petitions of prayer will never do the job. *It requires total life adjustment, individual and social.* Prayer and action go together. As a person prays, so he should act; and as he acts, he must of necessity pray.

—H. D. BOLLINGER

To Study Is to Serve God

Now there are varieties of gifts, but the same Spirit; and there are varieties of service, but the same Lord; and there are varieties of working, but it is the same God who inspires them all in every one.

—I Corinthians 12:4-6 (RSV.)

Lord, help me to be grateful for the privilege of study, for all the opportunities to discover truth for myself and to grow mature in mind and character, which academic work is offering. Help me to be grateful by using these opportunities rightly.

Help me to discover my proper place in all this: In the community of learning; in the fellowship of my friends and fellow students; in the vast field of knowledge which Thou hast opened before me; in the variety of gifts with which Thou hast endowed me; in the variety of services to which I may be called; and in the difficulties which may await me.

Help me also to discover my own abilities and limitations, but not to become proud of my talents. Help me to develop and use them in serving others.

I thank Thee, O Lord, for the living presence of Thy Son, Jesus Christ, in our midst. For Thy willingness to speak to me through Him and to guide me in my life as a student, I give thanks. For Thy promise that there is no truth without Thee and that all reality is one in Thee, I thank Thee. Amen.

—Peter Kreyssig

The major task of the Christian student is to be a student. He goes to his desk as to an altar. He studies with his whole heart and a single mind because God has called him to that vocation.

—Robert Hamill

17

THE CHRISTIAN VOCATION OF STUDENTSHIP

Do not be conformed to this world but be transformed
by the renewal of your mind, that you may prove what is
the will of God, what is good and acceptable and perfect.
—Romans 12:2 (RSV.)

O God, creator of this world and its truth, sustainer and redeemer
of students and universities, I would praise Thee and serve Thee
in the quality and integrity of my daily work—in class, laboratory,
library, conversation, in the papers I prepare and the examinations
I write—but I confess that so often I am conformed to this world
that I do not so praise Thee and serve Thee. Thus failing, I
need even more Thy loving forgiveness and grace.

I thank Thee, O God, for our Lord Jesus Christ and for His
gifts of transformation and renewal; for the possibility of proving
in my life what is the will of God for me; for the possibility through
Him of discovering that which is good and true and beautiful.
Accept this prayer, O Father, as confession and supplication, for I
pray that today and tomorrow I may take more seriously the
quest for truth, and understand what Thou callest me to do—
tomorrow and here today in this community. This I pray in the
name of my Lord and Savior, Jesus Christ. Amen.

—PARKER ROSSMAN

*The student who takes up the Christian vocation to student-
ship must take seriously the university as part of God's world.
He is called to be a Christian neither in spite of, nor in addition
to, but rather through being a member of the university community.*
—Wendell Dietrich

18

The Student Christian or the Christian Student

Live life, then, with a due sense of responsibility, not as men who do not know the meaning and purpose of life but as *those who do.* Make the best use of your time, despite all the difficulties of these days. Don't be vague, but firmly grasp what you know to be the will of God.
—Ephesians 5:15-17 (Phillips)

O Lord Jesus Christ, who filled Thy days with love and compassion and willing service unto the least of men, so enter into our lives, we pray, that we may become purposeful servants. Grant that as students we may begin each day with the offering up of our minds in obedience and service to Thee. Free us from enslavement to partial truths and distorted purposes which exploit the minds of men for power, prestige, or material gain. May we know and accept the corrective insight that comes from honest, open sharing with teachers and authors, and with fellow students who seek after Thy truth. Grant that the truth that rewards the diligent scholar and the wisdom that Thou alone canst give may find their true union in our lives. Amen.
—Harold H. Viehman

The contrast between that decent but superficial and schizophrenic fellow the student Christian, and that superbly integrated, and profound chap the Christian student is one which arose somewhere in the dark recesses of [The World Student Christian] Federation antiquity.

. . . it [This distinction] denies the possibility of a person being a Christian and a student with these two aspects of his life being unrelated. Either he conceives the fact that he is a student as a vocation from God, as providing the sphere in which he must discover and obey God's will, or he is not a Christian.
—A. J. Coleman

19

THE STUDENT IN POLITICS

> He purposes in his sovereign will that all human history shall be consummated in Christ, that everything that exists in Heaven or earth shall find its perfection and fulfillment in him. —Ephesians 1:9, 10 (PHILLIPS)

Almighty God, who by entering our world hast called us to service within the political life of the nations, we praise Thee for the redemption of the world from meaninglessness, for the demands of obedience in all areas of corporate existence, and for the examples of Christians at work in exacting positions of political leadership.

Forgive us for seeking the security of clearly defined moral positions, for blindness to Thy actions among the nations, and for our reluctance to follow Thee into the world of politics.

Lead us in new obedience that we may proclaim Thy sovereignty and purposes in political institutions on the campus, that we shirk not from serving Thee in political vocations, and that we always pray for Thy people in politics.

In the name of Him who has revealed Thy kingdom, our Lord Jesus Christ. Amen.

—ALLAN BURRY

The whole created order waits for the revealing of the sons of God, and every Christian's action in politics is a prayer, "Thy kingdom come, Thy will be done on earth as it is in heaven."
—M. M. Thomas and J. D. McCaughey

The University, the Christian Student, and Jesus Christ

> "As I passed along, and observed the objects of your worship, I found also an altar with this inscription: 'To an unknown god.' What therefore you worship as unknown, this I proclaim to you." —Acts 17:23 (rsv.)

Lord God of our fathers, who hast chosen to remain unknown even while from the very beginning of creation making Thyself known, readily do we kneel before Thee in worship and adoration. Emblazon us with the strickening character of Thy love that, being tossed about, we may with all vigor recognize Thee as He upon whom the concreteness of our situation depends.

Permeate our present learning with the constant awareness that always we stand before Thee, and that this posture hallows both our acquiring and our using of that which we gain here. May we with involvement of heart, toil of mind, and wholeness of strength make known to our university community who Thou art and how Thou hast reliably performed in and through Jesus Christ for the redemption of all life. It is by the grace of the Christ event we pray. Amen.

—Jim Lawson

The Christian student, therefore, is obligated to remind his university of the impact of Christianity upon the community which conceived, nurtured and prospered it; to show it that this larger community held some of the beliefs crucial to its conception because, and only because, in the days of its youth it knew this Unknown God made known in Jesus Christ, and that its life has always been informed by this knowledge.

To realize its purpose, the university must worship as well as work.—William H. Poteat

21

THE STUDENT'S PECULIAR SERVICE

> I delight in the law of God, in my inmost self, but I see in my members another law at war with the law of my mind. —Romans 7:22, 23 (RSV.)

Almighty God, Thou who canst turn the darkness into light, receive me now as I seek Thy face. Rebuke me not! but fulfill Christ's promise of compassion and mercy.

During these days in which I find myself a student seeking knowledge and truth, guide me, I pray, toward the truth as Thy light reveals it.

Amidst the confusion and complexity of the classroom and the fraternity house, assist me in retreating into my innermost being, that there I may find the meaning, joy, and quality of living which Thou hast given to life.

Give me strength and forbearance to do that which I believe, forsaking false leaders and expediency. Deliver me from the sin that is within my heart and reconcile me to Thee. Amen.

—JOHN WAGGY, JR.

By enduring the mental suffering of antagonistic theories and struggling to reconcile them into some coherent solution, the Christian student is sharing the life of Christ in his own vocation. This is the student's peculiar service unto God.—Robert Hamill

The Commuter Student

> Give your positive attention to goodness, faith, love and peace in company with all those who approach God in sincerity. . . . He must always bear in mind the possibility that God will give them a different outlook, and that they may come to know the truth.
>
> —II Timothy 2:22, 25 (Phillips)

Almighty God, Thou who art changeless though our vision of Thee changes, we who hurry too much pause now to worship Thee. We pause to thank Thee for the gift of Thyself to us in Thy Son, our Lord and Savior, and to enjoy the relationship that Thou hast thus granted unto those who love Thee.

In the quietness of this moment, the knowledge of Thy indwelling presence restores our souls and renews within us the desire to love one another even as Thou hast loved us. Forgive us for the times our haste has made fellowship impossible, our absorption in selfish concerns has caused us to ignore the lonely, and our submission to the pressures of job and family and grades has squeezed out of our lives the spiritual concerns and practices to which Thou hast called us. As we love Thee, enable us truly to love one another that our fellowship may be more meaningful; our vocation to studentship strengthened; our will to serve Thee on the campus, in the community, and over the whole world fortified. In the name of Thy Son, we pray. Amen.

—Fred H. Coots, Jr.

The commuter student, on the one hand, lives with one interest in a world of his home and the other in a world of the campus. By a daily process of alternation he takes out of each world what suits his purposes. . . . The college is a group of seekers and learners who are devoted to the highest development of the community and the persons in it.—Walter Muelder

THE CHRISTIAN STUDENT ON CAMPUS

The whole creation is on tiptoe to see the wonderful
sight of the sons of God coming into their own.
—Romans 8:19 (PHILLIPS)

O God, so often we become blind and insensitive to Thy creation—blind to the color of the out-of-doors, to the mountains, to
the sea, to the stars, and to Thy children. Let us not forget that
those who are created in Thine image are not abandoned by Thee—
that no matter how inhuman we become we are never outside of
Thy supporting love. Then, O God, make this security in love
purposeful by guiding our lives in the pattern of the Master.

Make active in us in the daily relationships of life the sacrificial
love that was in Jesus. Remold us to be sensitive to others, and
make us instruments of Thy healing power. Show others the
power of a life of quiet dedication. Remind us that this for which
we give ourselves belongs to the ages. In the spirit of the Master,
Jesus Christ. Amen.

—LOREN WOODSON

*. .The Christian student who would give something significant
to the world needs to begin by the spiritual discipline of his own
life in prayer, study and meaningful human relations on the campus.
. . . On campus the Christian will find innumerable paths leading
to all corners of the world, to all its depths of tragedy and to all
its heights of God-given possibility.*—Harold DeWolf

24

THE MEANING OF EDUCATION

The beginning of wisdom is this: Get wisdom,
and whatever you get, get insight.
—Proverbs 4:7 (RSV.)

Almighty God, who art the source of all life and light, we
are ever in need of that vitality and radiance which come from
Thee. May those who teach have sympathetic understanding of
the youth with whom they are privileged to share an understanding of opportunities and obligations. We pray that Thou wilt not
be far from teacher or student, for in the deepest sense we cannot
teach anybody anything. We can only help others learn for themselves, and without Thy continuing nearness the things we learn
may become delusions and snares.

Keep us ever mindful, our Father, that Thou art the potter, we
are the clay. For our troubled and questing spirits, we seek in-
spiration, comfort, and courage. Ever lead us as we seek to overcome our doubts, disillusionments, and frustrations with certainties,
joy, and hope.

May we be shepherds of the spirit as well as masters of the
mind; and may true learning always continue to be, as she has ever
been, the handmaid of highest faith. Through Jesus Christ our
Lord. Amen.

—CHARLES T. THRIFT, JR.

What education has to impart is an intimate sense for the
power of ideas, . . . together with a particular body of knowledge
which has peculiar reference to the life of the being possessing it.
—Alfred North Whitehead

EDUCATION IS AN ART

> "Hear, O Israel: The Lord our God is one Lord; and you shall love the Lord your God with all your heart, and with all your soul, and with all your might."
> —Deuteronomy 6:4 (RSV.)

O Lord our God, whose call in ages past was spoken to men so that they would know Thee and serve Thee, speak now to us Thy word of truth and life. Grant to us, we pray, an understanding of Thee so that we may be led to seek the spirit of unity in truth. Thou art the Truth whom we have seen in Christ—personal yet remaining mysterious, as near to us as our discipline, yet prompting in us the need to raise our eyes to Thee. Give to us the humility and courage to look into the depths of that which is ours to study, knowing that the truths we are led to uncover unfailingly point to Thy ultimate truth and illumine our limited wisdom.

Thou hast revealed to us in Christ that our lives become free for the quest for knowledge, for love of Thee with all that we are, and for service to all those who are given to us as our neighbors, only when we are bound to a knowledge of Thee which is self-dedicating. In the desire to offer ourselves, fulfill in us, we beseech Thee, that love which offers itself, even the love we know in the cross of Christ. Draw us toward such knowledge and devotion in all our learning that we may share the spirit of Jesus Christ, in whose name we pray. Amen.

—J. EDWARD DIRKS

Education is the guidance of the individual towards a comprehension of the art of life; and by the art of life I mean the most complete achievement of varied activity expressing the potentialities of that living creature in the face of its actual environment.
—Alfred North Whitehead

CHRISTIAN EDUCATION

The truth is that, although of course we lead normal human lives, the battle we are fighting is on the spiritual level. . . . We even fight to capture every thought until it acknowledges the authority of Christ.

—II Corinthians 10:3, 5 (PHILLIPS)

Our Lord, creator of all things and source of all truth, we ask Thy forgiveness for the sins of the mind; the pride of thinking that we are masters of creation and history; dishonesty and slackness in our studies; doubts about Thy power to make all things new. Cleanse our minds from unbelief and false doctrines.

Bless Thy Church, its institutions of education, its publications, its biblical and theological teachings. Bless especially our Student Christian Movements and their witness to Thy truth. Make use of us to proclaim the gospel and to lead all men to the knowledge of Thy love.

Come, Holy Spirit, and make our thoughts captive to Jesus Christ; in whose name we pray. Amen.

—PHILIPPE MAURY

A Christan education would primarily train people to think in Christian categories.—T. S. Eliot

THE CHRISTIAN ANSWER TO EDUCATION

Now if your experience of Christ's encouragment and love means anything to you, if you have known something of the fellowship of his Spirit, and all that it means in kindness and deep sympathy, do make my best hopes for you come true! Live together in harmony, live together in love, as though you had only one mind and one spirit between you.

—Philippians 2:1, 2 (PHILLIPS)

Eternal God, we praise Thee

for sending Jesus Christ, the way, the truth, the life; for the promise that we shall know the truth and the truth shall make us free.

Father, forgive us

for our failure to let our minds be a function of our whole being; for separating knowledge into watertight compartments; for allowing the breakdown of communication to separate us from our fellow students and faculty in other fields of specialization.

O God, give us

courage to pursue truth in freedom and with responsibility; concern for the ultimate values which give reason and scientific knowledge their true meaning; obedience to Thy will that Thy love may unite us across all barriers which keep us from the community for which Thou hast created us.

Through Jesus Christ. Amen.

—RUTH HARRIS

The Christian answer to the educational problem must be given in unity with the answer to the problems of personality and community.—Paul J. Tillich

28

RELIGION AND EDUCATION

Thus says the Lord: "Let not the wise man glory in his wisdom, let not the mighty man glory in his might, let not the rich man glory in his riches; but let him who glories glory in this, that he understands and knows me, that I am the Lord who practice kindness, justice, and righteousness in the earth; for in these things I delight, says the Lord." —Jeremiah 9:23, 24 (RSV.)

Lord of all power and light, author of wisdom, grant that all learning may be illuminated by Thy truth, all learners find their minds kindled by Thy understanding, and the communication of knowledge be redeemed by Thy love. Deliver us from false pride in knowledge and a futile trust that facts alone may release us from our bondage to ignorance and fear.

As we dedicate ourselves to Thee with mind and soul and strength, let the dedication of our mind bring true knowledge and just living, our dedication of soul be met by Thy presence in our lives and in our institutions, and the dedication of our strength bring matching power to set us free from our selfishness and sin. Through Christ our Lord we pray. Amen.

—DAVID SAGESER

If either religion or education is to fulfill its high mission in society, they must recognize their need of one another and join forces in common endeavor.—Paul J. Braisted

CHRISTIAN VALUES IN HIGHER EDUCATION

> Now the works of the flesh are plain: immorality, impurity. . . . But the fruit of the Spirit is love, joy, peace, patience, kindness, goodness, faithfulness, gentleness, self-control. . . . If we live by the Spirit, let us also walk by the Spirit. —Galatians 5:19, 22, 25 (RSV.)

Almighty and everlasting God, who by the Holy Spirit hast led men to establish colleges and universities for the advancement of true religion and useful learning and hast endowed Thy children with the capacity to learn and to do Thy truth, guide us in our search and study so that we seek not our own ends but Thine. Give us grace to know that the purpose of education is not for our own advancement alone, but rather to serve Thee in our several vocations.

Wherever we are, whatever we do, teach us to walk with Thy Spirit, serving and loving our brothers in the joyful knowledge that in this way we are following the example of Thy Son, our Savior, who came among men not as a leader but as a servant doing good. All these we ask in His name. Amen.

—PHILIP T. ZABRISKIE

As it seeks to become a community dedicated to truth and freedom, and as it seeks to develop critical, creative and responsible persons who will provide the much-needed leadership in society as a whole, the college or university must draw on its religious resources and develop its understanding of the place of Christian values in higher education.—Walter Muelder

Thinking Is Hard

Apply your mind to instruction
and your ear to words of knowledge.
—Proverbs 23:12 (rsv.)

Eternal God, Thou who hast placed us here as Thy children, we thank Thee for the sequence of events that have brought us to the university community.

Our Father, we confess that we have not loved Thee with all our heart and mind and soul and strength. We have been content with just meeting deadlines, with just fulfilling the law, with less than our best. We have looked for excuses to escape the rigors of study. Forgive us, Father, all that is past.

Help us this day to approach each book and each class hour with significant questions. From our hearts we ask Thee: Why are we here? Are our goals consistent with Thy will for us? Are we concentrating on the values that will endure? O Lord, give us the joy of a study life ordered by hard discipline. Deliver us from the desires for pleasure that lure us from our calling. Purge from our souls the elements of pride and jealousy. May our efforts this day prepare us for broader service.

Accept our study this day, O Lord, as our thank offering upon Thine altar. Accept our lives, O Father, as a living sacrifice unto Thee. We pray in the name of Jesus Christ. Amen.

—Don Kuhn

For now, you who live and breathe
Must do a harder thing than dying is:
For you must think
And ghosts will drive you on.
    —By an American soldier of World War II

CHRISTIAN THINKING

> Whatever is true, whatever is honorable, whatever is just, whatever is pure, whatever is lovely, whatever is gracious, if there is any excellence, if there is anything worthy of praise, think about these things.—Philippians 4:8 (RSV.)

Father of beauty, truth, and love, by whose goodness we are upheld and by whose truth we are nourished; lead us into Thy truth and teach us Thy courtesy, that relying on Thee we may learn to think in obedience to Thy will and by Thy truth be led into perfect freedom, through Jesus Christ our Lord. Amen.

Father, creator of our minds and of our spirits, who by the sending of the Holy Spirit hast given to us an inheritance with all the saints; cleanse our minds by the working of the Spirit and fill them with thoughts of whatsoever is pure, lovely, gracious, and excellent, that we comforted by Thy truth in this life may at last find eternal joy in Thy presence, through Jesus Christ our Lord. Amen.

—D. T. NILES

Every student's business in the academic community is to think, and the Christian's business is to think in Christian ways.

—Eduard Heimann

The Dedicated Mind

Whatever happens, make sure that your everyday life is worthy of the Gospel of Christ. So that whether I do come and see you, or merely hear about you from a distance, I may know that you are standing fast in a united spirit, battling with a single mind for the faith of the Gospel and not caring two straws for your enemies.

—Philippians 1:27, 28 (Phillips)

O God of grace, I bring before Thee this mind of mine with which Thou hast endowed me. By it Thou hast given me the gift of thought, the power to reflect and to choose; and because of it, I am not merely an animal but am called to be a unique instrument of Thy loving purposes. Save me, then, O God, from using my mind for unworthy ends which would degrade my fellow man and dishonor Thee.

Let the mind of Christ ever burn in me that I may exalt Thy name and serve Thy will as I search devoutly for truth. Help me to disavow shoddy habits of study and not to be casual or indifferent toward the fields of knowledge. This day and always I would dedicate my powers of intellect to Thy glory. In Christ's holy name. Amen.

—Ralph G. Dunlop

No religion can survive the judgment of history unless the best minds of its time have collaborated in its construction.

—T. S. Eliot

THINKING IS A FORM OF WORSHIP

> Do your best to present yourself to God as one approved,
> a workman who has no need to be ashamed, rightly handling
> the word of truth.   II Timothy 2:15 (RSV.)

We present ourselves unto Thee, O Lord, who hast first presented Thyself unto us. As through Thy grace Thou hast given us the gift of life and intellect, so through Thy truth Thou dost call us to glorify Thee with our minds. Forgive, by Thy graciousness, our intellectual sins against Thee; our pretension to know what we do not really know, and our neglect to seek out what we can and should know. Command us, by Thy truthfulness, to be honest workmen in Thine academic vineyard: to offer unto Thee conscientious service of mind and heart.

Lead us, O Lord, beyond knowledge to wisdom, and especially to that true wisdom which acknowledges that we, and all men everywhere, stand in need of the grace and truth which came from Thee in Jesus Christ, and come again in every Christly event. In Christ's name. Amen.

—FRED CARNEY

A Christian student should measure his love for God by first looking at his grade point. . . . Thinking is a form of worship, and the student's first business is to study. . . . The Christian student by the mastery of his studies can glorify God with his intellect.
—Robert Hamill

The Trained Mind

"For the sons of this world are wiser in their own generation than the sons of light."   —Luke 16:8 (rsv.)

Almighty God, our Father, who hast given us keen minds and
wills free to rebel against Thee, forgive us that we have so often
dedicated the power of our minds to the pursuit of worldly goals
rather than to loving Thee. Receive and accept these words of
thanksgiving for Thy wondrous gift to us in making us creatures
of reason, and also accept our confession of failure to use wisely
this gift. Forgive, cleanse, and restore us to the fellowship of those
who love Thee with their whole minds.

Grant that we may use wisely our opportunities as students and
scholars in the university community to grow in grace as well as in
wisdom, that our minds may lift us into the light of Thy presence
rather than lose us in the darkness of doubt, dispute, and despair.
Grant us that purity of heart which is to will one thing, that our
whole mind may be dedicated to the love of Thee and the pursuit
of the ends to which we are called by Thee. Amen.

—Glen O. Martin

The trained mind outs the upright soul,
As Jesus said the trained mind might,
Being wiser than the sons of light,
But trained men's minds are spread so thin,
They let all sorts of darkness in;
Whatever light men find they doubt it
*They love, not light, but talk about it.**

* From John Masefield's *The Everlasting Mercy.* Copyright, 1912, renewed 1940,
1947, by The Macmillan Company and used with their permission.

To Think Well

Prove me, O Lord, and try me;
test my heart and my mind.
—Psalm 26:2 (RSV.)

*Life is a continuous proving that there is an interior existence
trying to express itself in outward action. As I have tried to enrich
my inward life by thinking clearly and feeling deeply, as I have
sought to know when to speak and when to be silent because the
silence was more intelligent, I have realized more and more the
need to find my true home in the "interior court," where the spirit
of God can dwell and where it can speak and will speak if it is but
given a chance.*

Forgive me, O God, for having betrayed Thee in my inmost
self by crowding Thee out of my mind and pretending that I,
alone, should dwell therein. Give me, I pray, the sense of Thy con-
tinual proving, so that I may know Thee, and knowing Thee, understand. May this understanding be expressed in my life in whatever I do. This I want for my foundation. This I believe is Thy will.
Fulfill, then, Thy purpose in me that I may think well, that "the
eyes of my heart" may be enlightened, for I pray out of joy that
comes from feeling Thee in my "interior court."

—HAROLD EHRENSPERGER

To think well is to serve God in the interior court.

—Thomas Traherne

OUR THINKING MUST GROW UP

> The word of God is living and active, . . . piercing to the division of soul and spirit, . . . and discerning the thoughts and intentions of the heart. —Hebrews 4:12 (RSV.)

In the beginning, O God, Thou didst create the heavens and the earth; and then Thou didst create me in Thine image. That means that my mind was formed to seek Thee. My heart was made to know Thee. My whole life is most perfect when I am growing in my effort to become more like Thee.

I see the flowers pushing up through the melting snow and the fledgling bird trusting its untried wings. I feel Thy presence in my soul, which gives me an urgency to push beyond the places where I have been.

Help me to become more perfect by growing up. Help me to grow in my understanding, in my appreciation, and in my loyalty to the highest and best. Give me courage, vision, and a willingness to sacrifice. Give me a sense of Thy presence that I may stand firm and solid in time of stress. Help me to achieve a clear mind and singleness of purpose.

Thou hast trusted me in this mighty hour, and I dare not fail Thee. Save me from ignorance and sin. Help me renew my dedication to Thee that life's venture may take on a new purpose and deeper meaning. O God, unveil the poetry that has been ambushed in the prosaic, and help me to rise up like a man of God and be done with lesser things. In Thy spirit I pray. Amen.

—ORVILLE STROHL

. . . the world is now too dangerous for undersized minds. Our thinking must grow up, especially thinking with the recognition of right and wrong in it.—A. Powell Davies

THE CHRISTIAN COLLEGE

Yes, if you cry out for insight
   and raise your voice for understanding,
if you seek it like silver
   and search for it as for hidden treasures;
then you will understand the fear of the Lord
   and find the knowledge of God.
           —Proverbs 2:3-5 (RSV.)

Our Father, we thank Thee that Thou hast called us to love and serve Thee with our minds. Thou art pleased when we Thy children seek to know the truth, and Thou hast promised to guide us in the quest if we continue as Thy disciples. Help us, we pray, to keep the fires of the spirit burning during our college years. Raise up from among our generation of students men and women so disciplined by study that they will bring Christian insights into all the areas of knowledge. May they be able to dispel doubt concerning Thee and Thy plans and prevent this world from losing sight of the high aims Thou dost have for it.

Hear us in behalf of all who teach and all who learn, and may their lives be continually enriched by the wisdom from above. We pray in the name of Jesus Christ, our Lord and Savior. Amen.
           —JOHN O. GROSS

The aim of the Christian college is a community of rigor and reverence, of inquiry and worship, of competence and compassion, truth and love—an "atmosphere" of mutual acknowledgment of man's need for faith and his right to withhold commitment until honestly persuaded—Albert Outler

THE UNIVERSITY IS A MARKET PLACE

> The truth is that, although of course we lead normal human lives, the battle we are fighting is on the spiritual level. . . . We even fight to capture every thought until it acknowledges the authority of Christ.
> —II Corinthians 10:3, 5 (PHILLIPS)

Our Father, as we explore our faith through education and strive to extend our intellectual pursuits, help us, we pray, to employ our best abilities and talents in the Christian search for Thy truth. Confront us with the realization that an unfolding Christian discovery requires our most able resources, reason, and zeal. We would hold dutifully to this responsible and enlightened process of inquiry, recognizing that diligence, faithfulness, and disciplined growth are required in our search for Christian truths.

O God, we contritely confess our silence and inactivity about our Christian commitment. Any seeming inadequacy of the Christian faith to minister to the world's pressing needs is due to our failure to apply it to the great issues of the day.

Help us, we pray, that through the higher learning we may see the incompleteness of finite human experience as a sole determinant of life's richest, ultimate values. Give us grace to recognize that Thy infinite wisdom and reality convey meaning and purpose, widen our image of man and Thee, strengthen our concern, and sensitize us to unlimited moral obligation.

We humbly ask for insight and Thy guidance as we endeavor to apply, earnestly and effectively, our Christian ideals in the important daily decisions we face. We would have them witness to the essence of our faith. In Christ's name. Amen.

—H. R. RAMER

The university is a market-place and testing ground of faiths as well as facts.—Waldo Beach

THE NATURE OF THE UNIVERSITY

> "If you continue in my word, you are truly my disciples,
> and you will know the truth, and the truth will make you
> free."   —John 8:31, 32 (RSV.)

Humbly, we acknowledge, O God, that we are creatures in Thine eternal universe. We are grateful that this is not a finished world, but a world in whose continuing spiritual creation we are privileged to share with Thee. Though unworthy, we would fulfill this high trust. Forgive our faulty and feeble efforts, our sinful thoughts and motives. Creatively restrain us when our human wills would lead us into futile and destructive bypaths.

All that we have and are we rededicate to Thee, sincerely praying that we may in truth be human instruments freely serving in Thy divine employ. Help us ever to live as we pray, in the faith and spirit of Jesus. Amen.

—ED PRICE

The university belongs by its nature to the orders of creation. It is not an instrument for man's technique but one major means for entering a right relation to the created order. It is a channel of understanding in man who is in the natural order but transcends the natural order by his understanding of it. Its loyalty to God is manifest by its loyalty to God's ordering of things. Its duty is to truth and its work is the search for truth, defined as harmony with the structure of God's creation and the holiness of his will. Being responsible to God through his created order means being obedient to the laws of that order. The university does not find its community by obedience to anything partial within the created order, which includes the natural world studied through science, and the human world studied through history in all its dimensions.

—John W. Dixon, Jr.

Seeing God in Different Subjects of Study

"My thoughts are not your thoughts, neither are your ways my ways, says the Lord. For as the heavens are higher than the earth, so are my ways higher than your ways and my thoughts than your thoughts." —Isaiah 55:8, 9 (rsv.)

Eternal God, we praise Thee for all that Thou hast made. Grant us light by which to see our proper relationship to Thee as creatures. Free us from the prideful restraints which keep us from reverence. Shatter the self-sufficiency of fragmentary study, which leads us into idolatry. Broaden and enlighten our minds and warm our hearts by the teaching of Thy Holy Spirit.

We pray for a love of truth which will overcome desire for comfort in half-truth. Grant us the courage to venture beyond the easily seen landmarks of the subjects we love best. Open our eyes to the reality of Thy love in all its varied forms.

Let the mind be in us which was in Christ Jesus our Lord. Where vision is dim, enlighten us. Where courage is weak, strengthen us. Where devotion is halfhearted, revive us into that clear-minded search for Thee which moves along all avenues of truth. In the name of Jesus Christ, we pray. Amen.

—James Thomas

Each separate discipline of study, be it art or history or science, shows us something of the reality which is God. No one view shows us everything. The fullness of knowledge of God comes when we can place all separate revelations of Him side by side recognizing their differences and rejoicing in their complementary character, by which our knowledge of God becomes three-dimensional instead of two-dimensional as must inevitably be the case for any one view alone.—C. A. Coulson

SCIENTIFIC SKILL AND SPIRITUAL DISCIPLINE

> When thy judgments are in the earth, the inhabitants of
> the world learn righteousness.　　—Isaiah 26:9 (RSV.)

Almighty God, may we indeed believe that when we encounter reality in any way that we are finding Thee;

That in the classroom it is Thy work which we study, Thy laws which we learn, and Thy judgments which we confront;

That when disappointments come to us, Thou art seeking to strengthen and guide us as we encounter these painful experiences;

That when victories and pleasant places are enjoyed, they are not of our achievement, but of Thy grace and out of conditions which Thou hast established.

Grant us, we pray, the ability to see fact as Thy fact, and to accept ourselves as small parts of an existence greater than our pride, ambition, and preferences.

May Thy will have meaning to us, and may we seek it with all our strength and intelligence that in Thee we may gain stature as sons of God. Amen.

—BRYANT DRAKE

What we seek is a situation in which we so combine scientific and technical skill with moral and spiritual discipline that the products of human genius shall be used for the welfare of the human race rather than their harm and destruction.

—Elton Trueblood

Man's Spiritual Bankruptcy

> God has not given us a spirit of fear, but a spirit of power and love and a sound mind.
> —II Timothy 1:7 (Phillips)

Almighty God, who hast delivered us from the spirit of fear by the life and death of Thy Son Jesus Christ, we praise Thee for the abundant gifts of Thy Holy Spirit to us. For the power which keeps us from being more frivolous and faithless than we are and makes us more able to risk security and pleasure to serve Thee, we give Thee thanks. For Thine unfailing love, which casts out fear and fulfills the moral law and permits us to love one another in this world of strife, we praise Thee. For the soundness of mind, by which in diverse ways we can understand the perplexities of our time and bring all our concerns and works under the judgment of Thy manifest will, we thank Thee.

Forgive our misuse of Thy gifts, and enable us to offer them in faithful service to Thee, our only Lord and God. Amen.

—J. Robert Nelson

If the Church had claimed for God's service the new learning of the sixteenth century, if it had sought to baptize into Christ the new biology of the nineteenth century, or the new physics of the twentieth, how much alienation and estrangement from the Christian faith would have been spared today! What ruin and tragedy might have been avoided! Both the Church and the universities are paying dear for that fatal blindness. It will need great insight and humility on both sides to overtake the consequences. We must have collaboration on a new basis to rescue man from his spiritual bankruptcy.—F. R. Barry

43

The Meaning of Crisis

"I have set before you life and death, blessing and curse; therefore choose life, that you and your descendants may live." —Deuteronomy 30:19 (RSV.)

O God, our Father, Thou hast called us to live in a time of great crisis. We are aware of our inadequacies as we face the problems before us, yet we are thankful for the privilege of living in a day when the challenge is so great. In our confusion and lack of trust we often follow the way of those who would lead us deeper into tragedy.

Forgive us, O God, for our wavering faith and our unwillingness to place our trust in Thee. Make us to know the course Thou wouldst have us follow. Give us the courage to do Thy will in every situation, and the faith to leave the outcome in Thy hands. In Christ's name we pray. Amen.

—A. Darold Hackler

This is a day of crisis, but we do well to remind ourselves of that Chinese ideograph for "Crisis" which combines two ideas to make one word; namely, danger and opportunity.

—Bishop Herbert Welch

RIGHTEOUS RELATIONS

> I have been crucified with Christ; it is no longer I who
> live, but Christ who lives in me; and the life I now live in
> the flesh I live by faith in the Son of God, who loved me
> and gave himself for me.   —Galatians 2:20 (RSV.)

Father, forgive me when I think and act as though I myself am
the creator of Thy creation. Forgive me when in my daily decisions
I neglect both Thee and my fellow men as I place my own inter-
ests and opinions foremost. Forgive me when in the midst of my
busy schedule I fail to find time to give Thee thanks.

I am thankful for Thy gift of love and meaning which, through
Christ and the continued presence of Thy spirit, Thou hast revealed to me. Grant that in my renewed life born from this gift I
shall be filled with a spirit of forgiveness, love, and understanding.

In response to Thy love, I commit to Thee my talents and my
use of them in my home, my church, my own academic discipline,
and the wider world community. Amen.

—HERMAN CARR

*The Church is called in her lay members in the world to bear
witness to the good news of righteous relations which have been
conferred upon man in Jesus Christ. . . . The task of restoring a
sense of worth-whileness upon all men's activities.*
          —M. M. Thomas and J. D. McCaughey

The World Reborn

"Do not marvel that I said to you, 'You must be born
anew.'"　　　　　　　　　　　—John 3:7 (rsv.)

We come to Thee, our heavenly Father,
in simple childlike trust.

We praise and adore Thee for Thy
wondrous power and saving grace.

We thank Thee for Thy great Gift, Jesus
Christ, and that through unmerited favor
on our part we have become Thy children.

Grant Thy continuing favor upon those multitudes
who have as yet failed to surrender to Thy purpose
and will for their lives.

Forgive us, we pray, for our shortcomings—
for our sins of omission, commission, and disposition.

May Thy Holy Spirit direct us as we rub
shoulders with those who will run or ruin the world.

Bless all those who are playing the "sacrifice game"
that we may have this opportunity to learn.

Help us to let Christ have a fresh chance to
live through us today. In His name we pray. Amen.
　　　　　　　　　　　—William Hall Preston

This is our faith tremendous,—
Our wild hope, who shall scorn,—
That in the name of Jesus
The world shall be reborn!
　　　　　　　　—Vachel Lindsay

46

THE SPACE AGE

The heavens are telling the glory of God;
and the firmament proclaims his handiwork.
—Psalm 19:1 (RSV.)

Eternal Father, Lord of the heavens and the earth, as I pause in prayer to Thee, my heart leaps up at the thought of how great Thou art. Greater than the cloister can contain, greater than all the exclusive sectarian claims upon Thee, Thou art the God of sunshine and rain that falls upon the just and the unjust alike. Thou art the God of the sunset and wild flowers which awe the souls of Christians and pagans alike. But greater than all these things, Thou art my God who hears my prayers at this moment.

Now sings my soul, my God, how great Thou art! Amen.
—RICHARD A. BEAUCHAMP

. . . with silent lifting mind I've trod
The high untrespassed sanctity of space,
Put out my hand and touched the face of God.
—John G. Magee, Jr.

CHRISTIAN FRONTIERS

"Behold, the days are coming, says the Lord, when the city shall be rebuilt for the Lord."

—Jeremiah 31:38 (RSV.)

Read Jeremiah 31:31-40

Almighty and eternal God,
"who gives the sun for light by day
    and the fixed order of the moon
    and the stars for light by night,"
all praise and glory be to Thee for Thy creation,
and for Thy sustaining love.
I fail each day to keep the covenant,
by which Thou dost bind me to Thee in Christ.
Forgive my waywardness, O Lord;
put Thy law within me and write it upon my heart,
that I may know Thou art my God
and I am Thine.
Show me the service
that is my part in Christ's ministry this day
in each place that I am.
In the midst of this Thy world
let me stand in Thy eternal city
which can neither be uprooted nor overthrown.
"For thine is the kingdom and the power and the glory,
forever. Amen."

—ANONYMOUS

Christian students will see that the strategic problem is not where to draw the line of compromise, but how far Christian students can push the frontier of Christian control into yet unconquered territory.—Robert Hamill

Torment the Earth—and Exalt It!

"Do not think that I have come to bring peace on earth;
I have not come to bring peace, but a sword. . . . He who
finds his life will lose it, and he who loses his life for my
sake will find it."   —Matthew 10:34, 39 (rsv.)

O Creator and Redeemer of this realm, who hast given to us
Thy good earth for our joy and sustenance and hast set us free to
administer it in concert with our fellows; Thou dost know by
reason of our frailty and stubbornness we have grievously and
deceitfully used Thy presents. Grant, we beseech Thee, the gift
of Thy spirit of love that we may distinguish the wrong from the
right, the good from the evil; that we may with strength support
that which is necessary and with charity uphold the righteous.

Mercifully send Thy grace that we may be inspired to celebrate
Thy gift of life, in anticipation that all might live through Thy
Son who hast shown to us what life must be. Amen.

—Roger E. Ortmayer

*There's no turning back once I've spoken to you . . . because
it's your mission to torment the earth, and exalt it.*

—Maxwell Anderson

World-Mindedness

"The field is the world, and the good seed means the
sons of the kingdom."   —Matthew 13:38 (rsv.)

We are grateful, our Father, that through Thy grace we have
been called to serve Thee. We are continually called from sin to
faith and discipleship. Let Thy healing continue to make us whole,
and enable us to take our place in the university community as
Thy people.

When we have had insight into Thy nature, O God, we have
felt a divine imperative to share this with our fellows and to make
it known to the whole world. Our human weakness, ignorance,
selfishness, and prejudice sometimes keep us from making a faithful witness to Thee. For all of this, we ask Thy forgiveness. Help
us to have a more effective Christian attitude on the campus and
in the world.

Our world has become one; and at the same time it is broken
by war, hatred, economic strife, hunger, racial and national prejudice. Dear God, teach us the way of truth and life which Thou
hast provided in Jesus Christ.

We pray not only that we may know Thee, but that all mankind
in all the world may know and serve Thee. Our prayer is for all
our fellow students and faculty in every country.

Show us, O Lord, Thy will for our lives and let our little efforts
be for Thy kingdom and Thy glory. Lead us as students to be
about our Father's business. We pray in Christ's name. Amen.
                                        —Claude Singleton

Our destiny is to grow into world-mindedness. . . .
. . . The invitation of Christ's love is to communal sharing in
God's mercy and to that unlimited involvement in the burdens,
needs and blessings of other persons which constitutes Christian
world-mindedness.—Harold DeWolf

50

INDIVIDUAL WORTH—GOD'S GIFT!

He said to me, "Son of man, stand upon your feet, and I
will speak with you."   —Ezekiel 2:1 (RSV.)

Father, we praise Thee this day for all that Thou hast created
—the lovely and the unlovely, the majestic and the minute.

We bless Thee for the uniqueness of personality bestowed upon
each of Thy children. Grant us lucid insight into the divergent experiences and needs of those about us, that we may become appro-
priate means of Thy reconciling love in this world.

We invoke Thy strength for our own lives, O God, and ask
for Thy aid in the governance of our desires. Grant us the ability
to become witnesses of Jesus Christ, filled with humility, creativity,
and integrity.

In full recognition of our sinfulness, we ask for Thy mercy and
forgiveness. Restore us to Thy favor, O Lord, and fill us with Thy
grace. Amen.

—B. J. STILES

All I could never be,
All, men ignored in me,
This, I was worth to God.
—Robert Browning

A New Type of Man

> For if a man is in Christ he becomes a new person alto-
> gether—the past is finished and gone, everything has become
> fresh and new. All this is God's doing.
> —II Corinthians 5:17, 18 (Phillips)

God, we face decisions which baffle and perplex us. Often we appear casual and unperturbed, but there is a deep turbulence within us. Our decisions may not shake the world; but they may shape our world, the world of those about whom we care deeply.

In our heart we know that all of life is not of our making. All of life, including these decisions, is a gift. We know, too, that somehow Thou art the source of the gift. And we know both from our own hunger and from the way Thou didst make Thyself known in Jesus Christ that Thou dost offer a still greater gift. Thou wouldst make of us a new creation, a new type of man. Thou art in the midst of our life. Thou art in every decision, in every situation. Give us grace to open our lives to accept the gift. Amen.
—Bruce B. Maguire

What he [Jesus] desired was a new will, a new purpose, a new dominating impulse, arising out of one's loyalty to God, which should activate a new type of man, so revolutionary in character that this change was likened to a new birth.—Harland E. Hogue

A Better World—Better Men

> Put off your old nature . . . , and be renewed in the spirit
> of your minds, and put on the new nature, created after the
> likeness of God in true righteousness and holiness.
> —Ephesians 4:22-24 (rsv.)

O Father God, who hast made us and stamped upon our hearts and minds the image of Thee, we thank Thee for the gift of life. All that is within us rejoices that we may share with Thee the hope of a better world. Hold ever before us, we pray, the vision of a world without war, a human race without prejudice, a people who love their fellow men without fear.

We thank Thee for Thy dear Son in whose face and life we see Thy face—Thy life. We rejoice that in Him we have the perfect picture of what we, too, may become. We are grateful that we can now be better men than we ever dared hope to be—until we met Him. We are glad for this preview of the next great scene in the human drama—this glimpse in person of the Author and Producer of our Christian faith. Help us to see Him as the living Christ that He is. Pray give us the daring imagination to begin now the rehearsals for the mighty drama to come when we shall see Him face to face, as together we shall surely celebrate the inauguration of a new heaven and a new earth. In the name of Him—who loved this world and gave Himself to it, we pray. Amen.

—Howard W. Ellis

If we want a better world the answer is easy. We must have better men, and that begins with you.—Phillip Wylie

53

You're the Man

Let thy hand be upon the man of thy right hand.
—Psalm 80:17 (RSV.)

Eternal God, we praise Thee as students that Thou hast laid the hand of Thy calling upon us. Thou hast made us co-workers with Thee in our search for the truth of Thy universe. We thank Thee that Thou art ever with us in our quest and art ready to lighten our darkness.

Grant us, we beseech Thee, that we may be true to the trust which Thou hast reposed in us. Make us mindful of the sacredness of all truth because it comes from Thee. Cleanse our minds, lest we despoil pure knowledge. Lead us from knowledge to wisdom, and from wisdom to faithful devotion, that we may perfectly love Thee and worthily magnify Thy holy name.

We pray for the sake of Him who is the Truth, even Jesus Christ, Thy Son our Lord. Amen.

—R. H. Edwin Espy

We are ourselves in thought and voice—ourselves up to the very limit; and, consequently, if we want an Emperor, it's very clear that you're the man.—Henrik Ibsen

WHAT MEN OUGHT TO BE

For whatever a man may know, he still has a lot to learn; but if he loves God, he is opening his whole life to the Spirit of God. —I Corinthians 8:2, 3 (PHILLIPS)

Eternal God, our Father, we know that everything we are and possess is a gift from Thee. Everyone about us is a precious part of Thy world. As students, we have the special opportunity to delve deeply into the secrets of the universe, human life, and the whole plan and purpose of creation. But we are sinful sons and daughters, poor stewards of that time and talent entrusted to us. We are careless and superficial in our work, proud of our little achievements and oblivious of our many mistakes and shortcomings.

Help us to open our lives to Thy Holy Spirit, both that we may know what is Thy will and purpose for us and that we may be given the power to live as responsible Christian students—witnesses to Thee through our lives in this academic community. Help us, O Lord, we pray. Amen.

—JOHN JORDAN

It is only as men live near to the heart of God that they are able to sense the greatness of the distance between what they are and what they ought to be.—Everett Tilson

ONE THING

One thing I do, forgetting what lies behind and straining forward to what lies ahead, I press on toward the goal for the prize of the upward call of God in Christ Jesus.
                                        Philippians 3:13, 14 (RSV.)

O Thou one Lord of heaven and earth, Thou art the only source of all that I know and the One for whom alone my heart was made. Grant me that singleness of eye of which Thy Son spoke, so that knowing Thy forgiving and sustaining love I may have freedom from the bondage of shame and fear about my past; willingness to accept the responsibility of rectifying my past sin; courage to live in the present with its own tasks and dangers; wisdom to see the important in all the claims that come to me; and that love of Thee and every neighbor which judges all works by the obedient will of Jesus Christ.

I pray in the name of Thy Son, who with Thee and the Holy Spirit we worship as one God. Amen.

                                                —LARRY PLEIMANN

Purity of heart is to will one thing.—Soren Kierkegaard

OUT OF THE HEART

Keep your heart with all vigilance;
for from it flows the springs of life.
—Proverbs 4:23 (RSV.)

Our Father, we would love Thee with all our heart; but campus life so often surrounds us with influences that weaken our efforts. In our search for knowledge, it is easy to forget that wisdom depends on how well our heart will control the use of these facts.

Help us to take time out to commune with our heart and to establish a watch over our inner life and feelings. We would that our heart not trail the development of our minds and bodies.

May we avoid the faint heart or one that would fall in love with itself, but develop a heart that is fervent, sensitive, pure, enriched and enlarged with vision.

"Seach me, O God, and know my heart. Try me and know my thoughts, and see if there be any way leading to sorrow in me, and lead me in the enduring way." Amen.

—WILLIAM GRAHAM ECHOLS

If we have nourished the heart with good things, then more and more we want to do the right things.—James A. Pike

The Meaning of Salvation

"The glory which thou hast given me I have given to them, that they may be one even as we are one."
—John 17:22 (RSV.)

Our Father, we thank Thee for Thy whole creation. For the manifold evidences of Thy goodness around us, we praise Thee. We thank Thee that life with Thee has meaning. Most of all, we thank Thee for the realization of Thy love. Help us to know Thee better that Thy salvation may be revealed and made complete.

We would be worthy of the glory of Thyself revealed to us in order that we may share it with all Thy children, our brothers. To live divided in the human family is only to exist. Help us to realize our oneness with Thee and our brotherhood with all Thy people. Save us for this, in Jesus' name. Amen.

—Joe Bell

The purpose of the whole economy of salvation is to sum up all things in Christ and to enable mankind to share in the unbroken communion which the Son holds with the Father.
—Daniel Jenkins

Seek the Lord

"Seek me, and you shall find me; when you seek for me
with all your heart." —Jeremiah 29:13 (Moffatt)

Holy God, we who live in a strange city of bewilderingly rapid
social, political, technological, and intellectual change are faced
with forces that depersonalize, enslave, and destroy us. Blindly we
seek Thee, confused and knowing not what to do.

O Lord, help us to know that it is we who are blind, and not
Thee who art hidden. Assure us that we seek after Thee only
because Thou hast already found us. Be Thou our peace that we
may seek the peace of our city. In Thy holy catholic Church, by
word and sacrament confirm to us that Thou art Immanuel, God
with us. O Thou Lord of all life, be Thou the Lord of our life
through Thy Son, Jesus Christ. Amen.

—Herluf Jensen

*Perhaps the most important sentence in the Bible to our wistful
campus generation contains those haunting words to a distraught
people, so familiar to us through the Holy Week oratorio: " 'If with
all your hearts ye truly seek me, ye shall ever surely find me,' Thus
saith our God."*—Harland E. Hogue

READING THE BIBLE

All scripture is inspired by God and is useful for teaching the faith and correcting error, for resetting the direction of a man's life and training him in good living. The scriptures are the comprehensive equipment of the man of God, and fit him fully for all branches of his work.
—II Timothy 3:16, 17 (PHILLIPS)

Eternal God, we thank Thee for the Bible through which Thy Word is spoken to us and for Thy Holy Spirit by whom it is interpreted. Help us as we read this book to use our understanding, to wait upon Thy Word with love and eagerness, and to find the answer to our need.

Build us up in the faith, cleanse us of all error, show us the way of our obedience, and fit us fully for Thy work.

Through Jesus Christ the true and living Word. Amen.
—STEVEN G. MACKIE

Reading the Bible takes disciplined intellectual effort and mature spiritual appreciation.—Harland E. Hogue

What Purity of Heart Means

Truly God is good to the upright,
to those who are pure in heart.
—Psalm 73:1 (RSV.)

Almighty God, I would pray for purity of heart.

Many who have lived before me, and many who live this day, testify that Thou hast put into the midst of the existence which I share with all men the means by which I may know Thee and share Thy companionship.

They claim Thee to be the giver of all truth, the measure of all justice, the source of all love.

They give me Thy Word that I can know Thee as I center my living in Thy service.

They tell me of Thy promise that Thou art always near to share my life with me.

Be with me now and always—
that I may know that which is true,
that I may seek justice for all persons,
that I may share my common life with all
Thy children whom Thou wouldst have me love
even as Thou lovest me.

Turn me about that I may live in devoted companionship with Thee, that I may know of Thee—not only in the knowledge of my mind but that I may know Thee within the heart of my whole being. Amen.

—HARTLAND HELMICH

The "purity of heart" which Jesus makes the condition of knowledge of God equals singleness of mind, simplicity, essential integrity.—Alexander Miller

61

CHRIST AND CULTURE

"Either make the tree good, and its fruit good; or make the tree bad, and its fruit bad; for the tree is known by its fruit. . . . For out of the abundance of the heart the mouth speaks. The good man out of his good treasure brings forth good, and the evil man out of his evil treasure brings forth evil."   —Matthew 12:33-35 (RSV.)

Gracious Father, I acknowledge before Thee all the attitudes and actions of my life that are evil in Thy sight. Wouldst Thou forgive particularly my inclination to let the world mold me after itself. Come into my life with the Holy Spirit and cleanse me. Grant that out of my whole being might come, through Thy grace and favor, some fruit worthy of being called *good*. Transform my spiritual weakness into strength, my entrancement with the things of the world into rapture over the wonders of Thy kingdom, and my fondness for material values into an eternal love of Thee.

Out of the abundance of love which Thou hast bestowed upon me, let me speak with courage and faith for the transformation of culture and the proclamation of Thy love. This prayer through Jesus Christ, Himself the transformer. Amen.

—JAMESON JONES

Culture is the "artificial secondary environment" which man superimposes on the natural. It comprises language, habits, ideas, beliefs, customs, social organization, inherited artifacts, technical processes and values.—H. Richard Niebuhr

CHRIST IN US

"I in them and thou in me, . . . so that the world may know that thou hast sent me." —John 17:23 (RSV.)

O God, who hast called us to be Thy chosen people,
forgive us our many imperfections and our unworthiness;
purge us of those things which make it difficult
or impossible to see Thy good works in us;
be merciful unto us, O Lord, for our lack of responsibility
to ourselves and to all men.
We praise Thy name for manifesting Thyself to us in Jesus Christ
so that through Him we may know Thee more clearly.
We thank Thee for Thy Church on earth, for all faithful people,
and for the lives of the saints who have been before us.
We honor Thee for the vision which many have seen
or continue to see in working for reconciliation among people,
and in striving for the visible unity of Thy divided church.
We glorify Thee for all Thy manifold blessings to all men.
We pray, O God, for strength that we may in all things seek
to make Thy oneness known, and to demonstrate that in Christ
all barriers such as race, kinship, and color have been
broken down and are no more.
We pray Thee that we may have the courage
to unfurl the banner of salvation which Thou hast given us,
and that by lifting it up all men may know and worship Thee,
through Jesus Christ, Thy Son, our Lord. Amen.

—'BOLA IGE

As Christ is the mirror of God, so the church is the mirror of Christ. Either the world sees him in us, or it does not see him.
—Everett Tilson

THE CHURCH IN THE WORLD

"This gospel of the kingdom will be preached thoughout
the whole world."   —Matthew 24:14 (RSV.)

We give Thee thanks, O God, that Thy sovereign Lordship is
for the good of all men, that the proclamation of Thy kingdom is
good news. We praise Thee that Thy Son Jesus Christ promises
us that the gospel of the kingdom will be preached throughout
the whole world.

Lord, Thy promise calls us to share in Thy work for all men.
We are ashamed of our unfaithfulness. Grant us the strength for
full and joyful obedience. May we not be content only to preach
to all nations, but know how to proclaim the gospel in all realms
of life.

We do not know when the preaching of the good news will
accomplish Thy purpose in history. Thou alone, O Father, knowest
the day and the hour. We ask only to know that Thou hast given
to us the privilege of sharing in Thy marvelous work. Amen.

—VALDO GALLAND

*There is no New Testament Gospel except the world gospel,
and it is the claim of the New Testament that the mission of the
Church in the world offers a clue to the meaning of the history of
the world.*—Richard Shaull

THE CHURCH CAN ACT BEST

You are an open letter about Christ which we ourselves have written, not with pen and ink but with the Spirit of the living God. Our message has been engraved, not in stone but in living men and women.
—II Corinthians 3:2, 3 (PHILLIPS)

Our heavenly Father, we would be men and women who see things as they are, who call things by their right names, whose work is valid. We do not ask to be drawn away from everyday life, but to be in it with integrity and inner clarity.

We know, and Thou dost know, what is unclear, dishonest, shoddy, and self-deceiving about our lives. We are ashamed of these things; they are not what Thou hast created or willed. Forgive us this disloyalty to our neighbors, to ourselves, and to Thee. Open again the springs of inward health, and let the wholeness which Thou alone canst restore come to light. May the line from inner integrity to the daily vocation be clear for us this day. In Jesus' name. Amen.

—JOHN DESCHNER

The Church can act in the world best through the work of its members in their various vocations and as citizens.
—John C. Bennett

THE CHURCH—THE SPIRIT OF CHRIST

> You are fellow citizens with the saints and members of the household of God, built upon the foundation of the apostles and prophets, Christ Jesus himself being the chief cornerstone. —Ephesians 2:19, 20 (RSV.)

God, who so loved the world that Thou didst give Thine only begotten Son, Jesus Christ, to reconcile the world to Thyself, make us to understand our calling as ambassadors for Christ entrusted with Thy message of reconciliation. We confess that we have mistaken this privilege to mean that we can live in our church ignoring other churches and the world. Grant that we may strive for the fulfillment of Jesus' prayer that they all may be one that the world may believe, so that Thy churches, united and one, may show forth the spirit of Jesus Christ. Grant, too, that we may learn to be the Church from Monday to Saturday in our several callings, for in this the world judges the Church.

Come Thou, Holy Spirit, and fill Thy Church and us, because without Thee we are empty shrines with hearts that are cold, minds that are dark, and lives that are dead.

All this we pray so that we may be temples of Thine filled with the spirit of Jesus Christ. Amen.

—HARRY DANIEL

The community which carries the spirit of Jesus Christ through the centuries is the "assembly of God," the Church.
—Paul J. Tillich

66

GOING TO CHURCH

He [Jesus] went to the synagogue, as his custom was, on the sabbath day.   —Luke 4:16 (RSV.)

We thank Thee, our Father, for the privilege of worship. Make us mindful of those who cannot join us in praise, adoration, and confession today. Send Thy comforting mercies on all who are wracked with sickness or pain. Open Thou the windows of heaven to those who are in prison for conscience' sake. Deliver from danger all who risk their lives in dangerous labor. Bless those who labor today that we may have the creature comforts of life.

Save us from becoming too lazy to spend this hour with Thee. Deliver us from hypocrisy. Save us from making excuses to avoid our duties and responsibilities. Give us humble hearts to receive Thy Word, and help us to worship Thee with teachable spirits. In the name of Christ. Amen.

—VERNON BIGLER

Loyal participation in the worship of the church is the principal means whereby we keep alive and spread in the world the religion on which our ethic is based and which gives the resources for the Christian life.—James A. Pike

SALVATION IN THE CHURCH

> The time has come for judgment to begin with the
> household of God. —I Peter 4:17 (rsv.)

Heavenly Father, Thy wisdom hast given me, Thy child, a sense
of fellowship with Thee and with my fellows. Help me to know
the vitality of faith which has been the hallmark of Thy Church
through the ages. I am grateful that Thou hast set the solitary
Christian in the family of Thy household of faith.

May I find my continuing salvation through Thy continuing
revelation in Christ. Increase my willingness to be obedient to
Thy call on my life. Deepen my sense of humility as I receive
assurance of Thy love and care. Give me the genuine joy of in-
creasing knowledge of Thee through Christ, my salvation. Amen.
—HOOVER RUPERT

*The most effective way in which those who are within [the
church] can demonstrate to those without that salvation is to be
found in the church is by themselves living as humble, obedient,
and joyful servants of Jesus Christ.*—Daniel Jenkins

THE LIFE AND MISSION OF THE CHURCH

"Go therefore and make disciples of all nations . . . ;
and lo, I am with you always."
—Matthew 28:19, 20 (RSV.)

Our Father, Thou hast called us to make disciples of all nations
in the name of Thy son Jesus Christ. On our campus we have
representatives of the world Church. We ask Thy forgiveness for
the many times that we have failed to treat them as ambassadors
to us. We have ignored them and have been indifferent to the
message of Thy love which they could bring to us. Guide us into
an understanding of our responsibility as Christians to be concerned
for *all* Thy children everywhere.

May we find Thy will for our lives no matter where it will lead—
to the uttermost parts of the world or in areas of tension and need
at home. May we seek Thy redeeming love to serve Thee wherever
we are. In the name of our Savior, Jesus Christ. Amen.

—DOROTHY NYLAND

*Today we see several new factors in the life of the Church
around the world which demand a rethinking of its life and mission: the revolution in political and cultural life, the renaissance of
the non-Christian faiths, the rise of the ecumenical movement, a
new perspective on the church and its mission through biblical
theology.*—The Rangoon, Burma, Conference of the World Student Christian Federation, 1958-1959

THE CHURCH—GOD'S WORD

One thing have I asked of the Lord,
   that will I seek after;
that I may dwell in the house of the Lord
   all the days of my life.
                              —Psalm 27:4 (RSV.)

Dear Father, who art ever present in the fellowship of Thy people, make us evermore sensitive to Thy spirit in communion with those who love and serve Thee, so that we may be lifted above the wants and worries of self into that blessed company where Thy Word is the light and strength of life. Through Jesus Christ our Lord. Amen.

                              —BISHOP EDWIN E. VOIGT

Let Thy unwearied and tender love to me make my love unwearied and tender to my neighbor, zealous to pray for and to procure and promote his health and safety, ease and happiness . . . make me peaceable and reconcilable, easy to forgive, and glad to return good for evil. Amen.—John Wesley

The Church of God is born of God's Word, abides therein, and knows not the voice of a stranger.—John Knox

THE POWER OF A DEDICATED GROUP OF STUDENTS

"These men who have turned the world upside down have come here also." —Acts 17:6 (RSV.)

O God, who hast said Thou wilt be with any group which meets in Thy name; help us to move across our campus with a daring faith in Thy power to break down barriers and create good will. Unite us with our fellow Christians on this campus to really witness for Thee.

Keep us from the fear of being different. Give us courage to speak out for truth, justice, and brotherhood. Use our minds to seek new understanding of both faith and practice. Use our voices in classroom, dormitory, and church to bear our testimony to the power of Thy spirit.

Help us who live in a world of so much insecurity to give evidence of our faith by the lives we live daily on the campus.

In Christ's name we pray. Amen.

—G. EUGENE DURHAM

A group of fifty really devoted Christians who are not in the least apologetic and who are willing to make the spread of the gospel their first interest would affect mightily any campus in the country, no matter how great the initial opposition might be.

—Elton Trueblood

CHRISTIAN STUDENTS

"The place on which you are standing is holy ground."
—Exodus 3:5 (RSV.)

Almighty God, Thou who art always present but whom we too often ignore, we acknowledge Thy sovereignty. We humbly beseech Thee to forgive our sins, especially the sin of denying that Thou art Lord.

Help us, O Father, to realize the difference between being a student with Christian beliefs, and a Christian who is called to be a student. May we, with the guidance of Thy Holy Spirit, truly become Christian students.

Dear God, also help us to understand that we are on holy ground—ground that is holy because Thou art here. We pray that Thy divine presence may become a living reality in each of our lives.

We ask these things in the name of Jesus Christ, our Lord and Savior. Amen.

—JOHN CORSON

It is not enough to make students Christian. They must become Christian students. The place where they stand and where God has put them must be taken seriously.—Willem A. Visser 't Hooft

The Christian Witness to the University

> Till we should all attain the unity of the faith and knowledge of God's Son, reaching maturity, reaching the full measure of development which belongs to the fulness of Christ. . . . For He, Christ, is the head, and under him, as the entire Body is welded together . . . , the due activity of each part enables the Body to grow and build itself up in love. —Ephesians 4:13-16 (MOFFATT)

Our Father, we would grow in maturity. When we compare our lives to that of Jesus, we recognize how juvenile, how self-centered, how incomplete, and how much at loose ends we are. He, however, seems to have been so fully developed in spirit, so completely the master of Himself. When we ask why, we see the reason: He was fully surrendered to Thee so that Thy power and love and wisdom could be expressed through Him.

We would surrender ourselves also, Our Father—not to escape responsibility, but, rather, to prepare ourselves for more of it. To our learning, therefore, add wisdom, we pray; to our own creative power add love and sympathy; and temper our selfish emotions and passions with a great concern and respect for every child of Thine.

We ask this that we may grow to the fullness of Christ. Amen.

—LLOYD M. BERTHOLF

The Christian community is involved in the life of the university creatively and responsibly as well as critically. It affirms the true function of the university, calls the university again and again to its own purpose, and reminds it of its own ideal. In this sense the Christian witness is not just to members of the university but to the university itself.—Paul Deats

GOD IN OUR LIVES

" 'You shall have no other gods before me.' "
—Deuteronomy 5:7 (RSV.)

Gracious Father and Master of our lives, Thou who dost rule our generation with justice and love; we honor and hallow Thy name above all names.

We confess, O God, that our lives many times have not been worthy of Thee. We have failed to live righteously and devoutly because we have allowed unimportant and trivial concerns to crowd out supreme concerns. We have pursued our own pleasures rather than more complete fellowship with Thee. We have sought fulfillment in transient things rather than in Thee and Thy Church.

Forgive us for our faults and renew us for nobler living and deeper commitments to our Savior, Christ Jesus.

Our prayer is not for easier commandments, but for Thy grace and power to provide the dynamics to follow Thy present commandments. We know that a disciple of Christ must demonstrate his faithfulness by his deeds of goodness and by his high standards of morality. May Thy spirit create in us a hunger for righteousness and godly living so that our example may demonstrate the fullness of Thy presence in us.

Consecrate our purposes and our actions, that in both our plans and our deeds Thy mastery of our lives may be seen and Thy will be done. In Christ's name we pray. Amen.

—ROBERT REGAN

Christian ethics unequivocally starts with God; thus our first ethical duty is the exaltation of God in our lives.—James A. Pike

WORSHIP

"We do not know what to do, but our eyes are upon
thee."   —II Chronicles 20:12 (RSV.)

O God, as I turn my attention to Thee, I am overwhelmed by
the thought that already Thou hast turned Thine attention upon
me. In Thy presence, my pretenses melt and my masks become
transparent. It is no longer important that I am a man or a woman.
I am no longer impressed by my color, stature, features, or posses-
sions.

Here before Thee I am only myself. I am unable to pray selfishly,
or to seek personal favor. I am overcome by the gift of life, of love,
of faith, of courage, and of dreams. My heart is filled with gratitude.

Forgive me if I have trifled with that which is significant and
given significance to trifles. Hear my prayer for those who are indifferent to Thee, those who know not Thee, those caught in
tragedy, and those threatened by prosperity. Lead me in a plain
path today toward the accomplishment of the dream which is over
me. This I pray in Jesus' name. Amen.

—DRIGHT E. LODER

*Worship is . . . keeping related on a person-to-person basis with
God.*—James A. Pike

Prayer

> The prayer of a righteous man has great power in its
> effects. —James 5:16 (RSV.)

Eternal Spirit, Father of our spirits, we thank Thee that Thou
hast put in us that which reaches out after Thee as the plants reach
for the sun. Forgive us that knowing this we have all too often
neglected that by which alone we may grow and yield fruit.

Keep the pressure of Thy spirit upon us and teach us to pray,
that we may be possessed of Thee and fashioned by Thy will and
love.

As thus we pray for ourselves, let it not be for ourselves alone,
but for all the world. Deepen our understanding, enlarge our sym-
pathies, kindle our imaginations, and resolve our wills that we may
become instruments of Thy compassion and purpose and better
servants of the common good. Through Jesus Christ our Lord, we
pray. Amen.

—Paul Burt

*It [prayer] is the normal way by which man finds the unity of his
spirit with God's Spirit so that he may become an instrument of
God's creative energy and redemptive love.*—Thomas S. Kepler

ATHLETES OF THE SPIRIT

> Every competitor in athletic events goes into serious train-
> ing. Athletes will take tremendous pains—for a fading crown
> of leaves. But our contest is for an eternal crown that will
> never fade. —I Corinthians 9:25 (PHILLIPS)

Father, in whom we live and move and have our being, create
in me a clean heart, renew a right spirit, and guide me in the true
path of earnest endeavor, sacred trust, and a disciplined life forever. It is too easy to become delinquent with lazy habits. When I
am slothful in my ways, my mind becomes sluggish, my spirit of
striving ceases, and my desire to achieve vanishes—all fail. Therefore, I need a sense of purpose, a goal that I may know in what
direction I should be going. I need a clearer vision of what my
destiny is as a child of Thine.

But even with vision, almighty God, I must have power to cross
the goal line. This comes only from Thee, our source of life. As
Paul entreated us to "excel in everything," help me to have the
strength to match my muscles, the will to achieve, and the discipline to deliver myself worthily before Thee in everything I un-
dertake. Let Thy purpose and power be in me as they were in my
Lord, Jesus Christ. Amen.

—LEROY KING

We are required, therefore, vigorously to train as athletes of the
spirit to keep our lives constantly open to the power of God and
his guidance.—Harvey Seifert

77

GOD, THE FATHER

"The hour is coming, and now is, when the true worshipers
will worship the Father in spirit and truth, for such the
Father seeks to worship him."　　　—John 4:23 (RSV.)

Eternal God, our Father, who art the source of life and the
light of the world, we worship Thee in spirit and with glad hearts.
We praise Thee for the glory of struggle, the discipline of mis-
fortune, the wonder of love, the challenge of the highest values.
We bless Thee that through the Christ every worthy experience
is sanctified and becomes a sacrament of Thy grace.

We pray for an awareness of Thy divine presence. Thou hast
appeared to Thy children before: to the prophets of old, and in
the *Word* made flesh; Thou didst speak in earthquake and in the
still small voice. Visit us today with the joy of Thy presence and
the promise of Thy comradeship.

O God, create in us a right spirit that will make us teachable
and obedient to Thyself first, but also to those whom Thou hast
appointed to teach us. In our weakness give us strength. In our
ignorance give us wisdom. In our cowardice give us courage. Impart
Thy grace that we may follow the invincible Christ. Amen.

　　　　　　　　　　　　　　　　　—HARVEY C. BROWN

*God is not a power or principle or law, but he is a living, creat-
ing, communicating person—a mind who thinks, a heart who
feels, a will who acts, whose best name is Father.*—Robert Hamill

CHRISTIAN MARRIAGE

Walk in love, as Christ loved us and gave himself up for us, a fragrant offering and sacrifice to God.
—Ephesians 5:2 (RSV.)

Our heavenly Father, we are grateful for Thy provision that men and women should be attracted to each other, fall in love, and find in marriage a fuller life. We are thankful that Jesus taught us the importance of respect for personality, and that this has significance for us both before and after marriage.

We pray that in the choice of a mate Christian concern may rule our minds as well as our hearts. May our marriage be based upon the high ideals and teachings of our Lord and Savior, Jesus Christ, so that we will not hurt each other in marriage, but may grow together in Christian love and fellowship, "till death us do part." Amen.

—EDWARD D. STAPLES

Christian marriage is primarily an act of the will. It is born in love, nourished in growing affection, but it matures in faithfulness.
—Robert Hamill

OUR LIFE IS LENT TO BE SPENT

"He who loves his life loses it, and he who hates his life
in this world will keep it for eternal life."
—John 12:25 (RSV.)

Today again, Lord, the Holy Spirit has enkindled in me the
keen desire to follow Thee from morning to evening, as once did
Thy disciples.

But may the requirements of Thy Word not stop me on my way
of following Thee, if Thou callest me suddenly to lose my life in
a great or small sacrifice!

Teach me, then, Lord, not to fear the trial, for it is Thee who,
from morning to evening, accompaniest me in the detours of my
road.

Teach me, then, Lord, to lose my selfish will in the peace of the
heart Thou dost give, because every word from Thy lips guides me
toward the resurrection; teach me to hate without anguish my
narrowness, for it is Thee who sustainest me ceaselessly in giving
me my fellow man for companionship.

May I not falter today, Lord, and may my desire to follow Thee
increase at each step through the grace of the Holy Spirit! Amen.
—CYRILLE ELTCHANINOFF

*It is through dying to concern for self that we are born to a new
life with God and others; in such dying and rebirth, we find that
our life is lent to be spent; and in such spending of what we are
lent, we find there is an infinite supply.*—Glenn Olds

IN THE PRESENCE OF GOD

"If the Lord is God, follow him."—I Kings 18:21 (RSV.)

O God, our Father, Thou who art the God of Abraham, Isaac and Jacob, and the God of Jesus Christ, our Lord, we adore Thee. We give thanks to Thee because Thou art the God of our fathers, the prophets and the apostles, the God of the ancient people of Israel and the church of today. Thou art the God of the Bible, the creator of the universe, who hast visited men. We know that Thou art God and not man, but God who became as one of us in Jesus that we might know Thee and live in Thee.

We beseech Thee to keep us courageous in our faith and faithful to Thee as were Thy servants of the past, who though misunderstood and persecuted, yet remained faithful unto death and received the crown of life.

In the university, we are witnesses to the unconcern and disdain of those who do not believe in Thee; to the presence of those who take Thy name, but do not follow Thee; to the challenge of a world proud of its civilization and science, confident in the progress of its technique, but afraid of the future, without peace, without hope. Be with us, O Lord! Create in us strength of mind, humbleness of heart, and submission of our will to Thy will so that we may serve Thy purpose and proclaim the good news of salvation. Through Jesus Christ our Lord. Amen.

—JORGE CESAR MOTA

"When we . . . trace the most essential part of religion back to its most essential element, we find a man standing in the presence of God . . . ready to declare in the teeth of all opinion and all persecution, "Thus saith the Lord."—H. Wheeler Robinson

81

WHEN IS A MAN SAVED?

" 'I will arise and go to my father.' "—Luke 15:18 (*RSV*)

O gracious and loving Father, I turn to Thee in my hour of crisis, even as a wilful son who has squandered his inheritance, dishonored his family, and lost his way. I am bewildered, uncertain, ashamed, and poor indeed.

I beseech Thee, O God, who art all-wise, all-powerful, and who lovest me in spite of all my short comings and unworthiness, to hear the cry of my anguished heart and restore my soul. Cleanse my thoughts and renew a pure mind within me. Reveal Thy lofty plan for my life and give me a holy purpose, for I stand in sore need of both faith and courage.

I humbly renounce all the selfish desires for pleasures which have impoverished my body, mind, and spirit; I solemnly vow to surrender my life wholly to Thee. From this time henceforth I promise to dedicate my time, my talents, and my treasure in love of Thee and to the service of my fellow man. Amen.

—WILLIAM J. FAULKNER

When is a man saved? When, in surrender to God, he finds release from the tyranny of self to find freedom in the service of mankind. Thus he is converted to pursuit of the ends for which he was created. That is why he sometimes speaks of salvation as self-discovery; man was made for God. We are saved, as was the Prodigal Son, when we come to ourselves and give up to our Father.—Everett Tilson

WHAT IS VITAL RELIGION?

He has showed you, O man, what is good;
    And what does the Lord require of you
but to do justice, and to love kindness,
    and to walk humbly with your God?
                    —Micah 6:8 (RSV.)

Most gracious Lord, Thou alone art the all-wise creator of life.

To Thee we address our fretful cries for revelation as we find our course through uncertainties and frustrations of our daily lives. Without the privilege of communion with Thee, O Lord, there is no reality to the swiftly passing stream in which we live.

We are deeply grateful for Thy divine being. In Thee we find the compelling force of love which shapes our growth in Thy service. Grant that we may be increasingly aware of Thy presence within us, that gives to us the spiritual strength and sense of vitality with which we may face the world as sons of Thine, constant in prayer, walking in the way of righteousness and humility before Thy majesty. Amen.

                    —GERRY McCULLOH, JR.

What is real and vital religion? The biblical answer is personal encounter between Spirit and spirit, a living dialogue between Person and person, man's never-ending adventure with God.

                    —Everett Tilson

THE MEANING OF WORSHIP

How lovely is thy dwelling place
O Lord of hosts!
My soul longs, yea, faints
for the courts of the Lord;
my heart and flesh sing for joy
to the living God.
—Psalm 84:1, 2 (RSV.)

O Thou who art holy, I raise to Thee my heart and soul in joy and thanksgiving. I thank Thee that Thou art not as man—weak, vacillating, shortsighted, short-lived. Were Thou thus, I could but despair. But my hope and joy is in coming into the beauty of Thy holiness, into the presence of Thine eternity to seek Thy truth and Thy will for my life.

Take away, I pray Thee, those barriers of pride and self-will which keep me from the loveliness of Thy dwelling place; and lift me to ever higher planes of activity and purpose. All this I dare to bring before Thee, O holy One, in the name of Him who showed me who and what Thou art. Amen.

—DOT AND BILL ANDERSON

To worship is to quicken the conscience by the Holiness of God, to feed the mind with the truth of God, to purge the imagination by the beauty of God, to open the heart to the love of God, to devote the will to the purpose of God. All this is gathered up in that emotion which most cleanses us from selfishness because it is the most selfless of all emotions—Adoration.—William Temple

Make Me New

Create in me a clean heart, O God,
  and put a new and right spirit within me.
                      —Psalm 51:10 (RSV.)

O God, Thou hast searched us and known us, and art acquainted with all our ways. Thou dost understand us better than we understand ourselves. Thy love hast supported us through all our days, and even now calls us to turn to Thee.

We thank Thee for Thy mercy and forgiveness in the face of our great need. We confess that we are:
  lenient with our own faults,
  severe with the faults of others;
  complacent in times of great blessing,
  faithless in time of disappointment;
  attentive to trivia,
  careless in the great work of Thy kingdom.

Recall us to Thyself, O Lord. Take firm hold of our lives that we may never turn from Thee. Cleanse and renew us for lives of discipleship; through Jesus Christ our Lord. Amen.
                      —R. Jerrold Gibson

Batter my heart, three-personed God; for you
As yet but knock; breathe, shine and seek to mend;
That I may rise and stand, o'erthrow me, and bend
Your force, to make, blow, burn, and make me new.
                      —John Donne

FAITH

> Take your stand then with truth as your belt, righteousness your breastplate, the Gospel of peace firmly on your feet, salvation as your helmet and in your hand the sword of the Spirit, the Word of God. Above all be sure you take faith as your shield. —Ephesians 6:14-16 (PHILLIPS)

Almighty God, our loving heavenly Father, we thank Thee that we can depend on Thy faithfulness. When troubles beset us, when calamities and chaos increase on all sides, merciful Father, grant us confidence in Thee. Holy Father, when we are worried and anxious about our future, grant us faith to trust that the future belongs to Thee and we are safe in Thee.

O Lord Jesus Christ, who promised, "Lo, I am with you always, even unto the end of the world," grant us grace to believe Thy promises. O Thou who art the same yesterday, today and forever, give us faith to believe that Thou art our Lord and the Lord of the whole world.

O God, the Holy Spirit, give us grace to trust that Thou art the giver of life and that Thou art in our midst guiding us to Thy purposes. Grant us faith to believe that victory belongs to Thee.

O God, the Father, Son, and the Holy Spirit, grant us, Thy feeble and faithless children, grace to trust Thee completely and to abandon ourselves uttterly into Thy hands. We commit our desires, hopes and aspirations, our loved ones and their welfare into Thy care. Whatever happens, Thou art our God, and we are Thine. Take us, use us for Thy glory, for we ask in the name and for the sake of Jesus Christ our Lord. Amen.

—P. T. THOMAS

Faith is a totality-act of the whole personality.—Emil Brunner

ADVENTURE—WIN OR LOSE

"The people who know their God shall stand firm and
take action."　　　　　　　—Daniel 11:32 (RSV.)

Eternal God, our Father, who hast created the family of mankind to dwell in fellowship and hast manifested before all the nations the victory of Thy love upon the cross, accept the quiet resolve of my heart to place my life at Thy service. Perfect, O Lord,
the talents Thou hast given me; chasten the impure, self-centered
striving of my rebellious spirit; forge into resilient steel my will to
follow Thee no matter what the cost; and direct my feet wherever
Thou needest my witness.

I ask no favor but to glorify Thy name. I ask no success but to
give my all for Thy kingdom, no recompense but the knowledge
that Thou art with me. Even though the forces of evil may rise up
against me and earthly hopes be frustrated, give me joy in the
knowledge that I am serving Thee, and that the final victory is
Thine. This I pray in Jesus' name. Amen.

—RAIMUNDO VALENZUELA

*. . . a man is saved when he says "yes" to God; that his life is a re-
sponse to something that has happened to him and never again
does he count the cost, but dares to throw his life upon the great
adventure, win or lose.*—Gerald Kennedy

ACKNOWLEDGMENTS

We express grateful appreciation to the following for permission to reprint materials as follows:

Abingdon Press, Nashville, for quotations from *Christian Faith and the Campus Mind* by Harland E. Hogue; *Fellowships of Concern* by Harvey Seifert; and *Gods of the Campus* by Robert Hamill.

The Methodist Student Movement, Department of College and University Religious Life, Board of Education, Nashville, for quotations from *Art As Communication* by John W. Dixon, Jr.; *Credo* by Thomas S. Kepler; *The Christian Corrective to the Campus Confusion* by Glenn Olds; *The Conscience of Culture* by Everett Tilson; *The Responsible Student* by Harold Ehrensperger and others; and *Worship and the Arts* by Keith Irwin and Roger Ortmayer.

The World's Student Christian Federation, Geneva, Switzerland, for quotations from *The Christian in the World Struggle* by M. M. Thomas and J. D. McCaughey; and the quotation from A. J. Coleman's book *The Task of the Christian in the University,* published by Association Press.

The Student Christian Movement Press Limited, London, for the quotation by William Temple from his book *The Hope of a New World,* published by The Macmillan Company.

The Association Press, New York, for quotations by Waldo Beach, William H. Poteat, and Wendell Dietrich from *The Christian Student and the University,* edited by J. Robert Nelson; quotation by Eduard Heimann from *The Christian Student and World Struggle,* edited by J. Robert Nelson; and the quotation from *Encounter with Revolution* by M. Richard Shaull.

Beacon Press, Boston, for quotations by A. Powell Davies and Gerald Kennedy, from *Sermons from an Ecumenical Pulpit,* edited by Max F. Daskam.

Doubleday and Company, Inc., New York, for quotations from *The Renewal of Man* by Alexander Miller (copyright ©, 1955 by the author); *The Strangeness of the Church* by Daniel Jenkins, copyright ©, 1955 by the author; and *Doing the Truth* by James A. Pike.

Harper and Brothers, New York, for quotations from *The Predicament of Modern Man* by Elton Trueblood, copyright, 1944; *The Moffatt Bible: A New Translation* by James Moffatt, copyright by Harper and Brothers 1922, 1935, and 1950.

Mrs. John G. Magee, for the quotation from the poem "High Flight," by her son John G. Magee, Jr.

The Macmillan Company, New York, for quotations from *The New Testament in Modern English* by J. B. Phillips, copyright, 1958; the quotation from Vachel Lindsay's poem "Foreign Missions in Battle Array," from *Collected Poems*, copyright, 1925; the quotation from John Masefield's narrative poem "The Everlasting Mercy" from his book *The Everlasting Mercy*, copyright, 1912 and renewed in 1940 and 1947 by The Macmillan Company; and quotations from *Aims of Education and Other Essays* by Alfred North Whitehead, copyright, 1929 by The Macmillan Company and renewed, 1957 by Evelyn Whitehead.

Dr. Albert Outler of Perkins School of Theology, Dallas, Texas, for his quotation which was published in *Information Service*, February 14, 1959.

The Philosophical Library, Inc., New York, for the quotation by C. A. Coulson from *An Approach to Christian Education*, edited by Rupert E. Davies.

Charles Scribner's Sons, New York, for quotations by F. R. Barry from his book *The Recovery of Man*, copyright, 1949; John C. Bennett from his book *Christian Ethics and Social Policy*; and Paul J. Tillich from *The Christian Answer*, edited by Henry P. Van Dusen.

We are especially grateful to Miss Margaret Rigg of the *motive* staff for the emblem on the cover.

The Scripture quotations indicated by the abbreviation (RSV.) are from the Revised Standard Version of the Holy Bible, copyrighted by the Division of Christian Education of the National Council of the Churches of Christ in the United States of America.

Additional Helps

Book of Student Prayers, by Jack Finegan, Association Press, New York.

The Student Prayerbook, arranged by John Oliver Nelson, Association Press, New York.

Student Prayer, Student Christian Movement Press, London, England.

A Devotional Diary, arranged by J. H. Oldham, Richard R. Smith, Inc., New York.

AUTHORS OF QUOTATIONS

CONTRIBUTORS

ANDERSON, DOT AND BILL: Missionaries in Cambine, Mozambique, Portuguese East Africa. (84)*

ANONYMOUS (48)

BEAUCHAMP, RICHARD A.: Student at Randolph-Macon College, Ashland, Virginia, (47)

BELL, JOE: Director of Youth Department, Board of Education of The Methodist Church, Nashville, Tennessee. (58)

BERTHOLF, LLOYD M.: President, Illinois Wesleyan University, Bloomington, Illinois. (73)

BIGLER, VERNON: Minister, Terre Haute, Indiana. (67)

BROWN, HARVEY C.: Director of Higher Education in Wesley Foundations, Board of Education of The Methodist Church, Nashville, Tennessee. (78)

BURRY, ALLAN: President, National Student Christian Federation. (20)

BURT, PAUL: Pastor-Director, Wesley Foundation, University of Illinois, Urbana, Illinois. (76)

CARNEY, FRED: Professor, Perkins School of Theology, Dallas, Texas. (34)

CARR, HERMAN: Assistant Professor of Physics, Rutgers University, New Brunswick, New Jersey. (45)

COOTS, FRED H, JR.: Pastor, Monterey Park, California. Formerly, National Student Chairman of the Y.M.C.A. (23)

CORSON, JOHN: Former President, National Conference of Methodist Youth. (72)

DANIEL, HARRY: General Secretary, Student Christian Movement of India. (66)

DESCHNER, JOHN: Associate Professor of Theology, Perkins School of Theology, Dallas, Texas, and Chairman of the Executive Committee of the National Student Christian Federation. (65)

* Number in parentheses gives page of contributor's prayer.

DIRKS, J. EDWARD: Professor of Christian Methods, Yale University Divinity School, New Haven, Connecticut, and Editor of *The Christian Scholar*. (26)

DRAKE, BRYANT: National Secretary, Campus Ministry, United Church of Christ, La Grange, Illinois. (42)

DUNLOP, RALPH G.: Chaplain, Northwestern University, Evanston, Illinois. (33)

DURHAM, G. EUGENE: Pastor, Palmyra, New York. Thirty-five years a Minister to Students at Cornell and Northwestern universities. (71)

ECHOLS, WILLIAM GRAHAM: Twenty-five years Director of the Wesley Foundation at the University of Alabama, University, Alabama. (57)

EHRENSPERGER, HAROLD: Associate Professor of Religion, Boston University School of Theology, Boston, Massachusetts. Former Editor of *motive*. (36)

ELLIS, HOWARD W.: Director, Cooperative Department of Youth Evangelism, the General Board of Evangelism of The Methodist Church, Nashville, Tennessee. (53)

ELTCHANINOFF, CYRILLE: General Secretary, Russian Student Christian Movement Outside Russia, Paris, France. (80)

ESPY, R. H. EDWIN: Associate General Secretary, the National Council of the Churches of Christ in the U. S. A., New York, N. Y. Formerly, General Secretary of the Student Y.M.C.A. (54)

FAULKNER, WILLIAM J.: Former Dean of the Chapel at Fisk University. Presently, at The Congregational Church of Park Manor, Chicago, Illinois. (82)

GALLAND, VALDO: Associate General Secretary, World Student Christian Federation. (64)

GIBSON, R. JERROLD: Director, Wesley Foundation at Harvard University, Cambridge, Massachusetts. (85)

GROSS, JOHN O.: General Secretary, Division of Higher Education, Board of Education of The Methodist Church, Nashville, Tennessee. (38)

HACKLER, A. DAROLD: Director of Wesley Foundation at Ohio State University, Columbus, Ohio. (44)

HARRIS, RUTH: National Student Secretary, Woman's Division of Christian Service, Board of Missions of The Methodist Church, New York, N. Y. (28)

HELMICH, HARTLAND: National Secretary, Campus Ministry, United Church of Christ. (61)

IGE, 'BOLA: Co-Secretary of the 18th Ecumenical Student Conference on the Christian World Mission. Formerly, the General Secretary of the Student Christian Movement in Nigeria. (63)

JENSEN, HERLUF: Executive Secretary, National Student Christian Federation, New York, N. Y. (59)

JONES, JAMESON: Editor, *motive*, Magazine of The Methodist Student Movement, Board of Education of The Methodist Church, Nashville, Tennessee. (62)

JORDAN, JOHN: Student, Drew Theological Seminary, Madison, New Jersey. Former Rhodes Scholar. (55)

KING, LEROY: Pastor, Denver, Colorado. Former basketball star at Northwestern University and professional basketball player with the Rochester Royals. (77)

KREYSSIG, PETER: General Secretary of the Student Christian Movement of Germany. (17)

KUHN, DON: Admissions Counselor, Garrett Biblical Institute, Evanston, Illinois. (31)

LAWSON, JIM: Southern Regional Secretary of the Fellowship of Reconciliation. (21)

LODER, DWIGHT E.: President, Garrett Biblical Institute, Evanston, Illinois. (75)

MACKIE, STEVEN G.: Editor of *The Student Movement*, and Study Secretary, Student Christian Movement of Great Britain and Ireland. (60)

MAGUIRE, BRUCE B.: Executive, National Student Council of Y.M.C.A.'s. (52)

MARTIN, GLEN O.: Director of Wesley Foundation and also the School of Religion, University of Tennessee, Knoxville, Tennessee. (35)

MAURY, PHILIPPE: General Secretary, World Student Christian Federation. (27)

McCULLOH, GERRY, JR.: Student at Vanderbilt University, Nashville, Tennessee. (83)

MOTA, JORGE CESAR: Secretary of Publications, Student Christian Movement of Brazil. (81)

NELSON, J. ROBERT: Former Dean of the Divinity School, Vanderbilt University, Nashville, Tennessee. (43)

NILES, D. T.: Chairman of the Executive Committee, World Student Christian Federation. (32)

NYLAND, DOROTHY: Secretary of Promotion, The Women's Guild of the Evangelical and Reformed Church. (69)

ORTMAYER, ROGER E.: Professor of Christianity and the Arts, Perkins School of Theology, Dallas, Texas. Former Editor of *motive*. (49)

PLEIMANN, LARRY: Student at Perkins School of Theology, Dallas, Texas. Formerly, Chairman, National Methodist Student Commission. (56)

PRESTON, WILLIAM HALL: Staff Associate, Student Department, Education Division, the Sunday School Board of the Southern Baptist Convention, Nashville, Tennessee. (46)

PRICE, ED: Since 1920, Director of the Wesley Foundation at the University of Kansas, Lawrence, Kansas. (40)

RAMER, H. R.: Director of the International House, Ohio State University, Columbus, Ohio. (39)

REGAN, ROBERT: Director, Department of Organizational Activities, The Board of Christian Concerns of The Methodist Church, Washington, D. C. Former Wesley Foundation Director. (74)

ROSSMAN, PARKER: Associate Professor of Religion in Higher Education, Yale University Divinity School, New Haven, Connecticut. (18)

RUPERT, HOOVER: Pastor, Ann Arbor, Michigan. (68)

SAGESER, DAVID: Pastor, Cincinnati, Ohio. Formerly, Executive Director, Department of Campus Christian Life, National Council of the Churches of Christ. (29)

SINGLETON, CLAUDE: Director, Department of Student Work, Board of Missions of The Methodist Church, New York, N. Y. (50)

STAPLES, EDWARD D.: Director, Department of the Christian Family, Board of Education of The Methodist Church, Nashville, Tennessee. (79)

STILES, B. J.: Associate Director, Department of College and University Religious Life, Board of Education of The Methodist Church, Nashville, Tennessee. (51)

STROHL, ORVILLE: President, Southwestern College, Winfield, Kansas. (37)

THOMAS, JAMES: Associate Director, Department of Secondary and Higher Education, Division of Educational Institutions, Board of Education of The Methodist Church, Nashville, Tennessee. (41)

THOMAS, P. T.: Graduate Student, University of Chicago, Chicago, Illinois. Formerly, on the staff of the Student Christian Movement of India. (86)

THRIFT, CHARLES T., JR.: President, Florida Southern College, Lakeland, Florida. (25)

VALENZUELA, RAIMUNDO: Senior Advisor, Student Christian Movement in Chile. (87)

VIEHMAN, HAROLD H.: Former Secretary, Department of Campus Christian Life, Board of Christian Education of the United Presbyterian Church. (19)

VOIGT, BISHOP EDWIN E.: Dakota Area, The Methodist Church, Aberdeen, South Dakota. (70)

WAGGY, JOHN, JR.: Student, Yale University Divinity School, New Haven, Connecticut. Formerly, Chairman, National Methodist Student Commission. (22)

WOODSON, LOREN: Student, Pomona College, Claremont, California. (24)

ZABRISKIE, PHILIP T.: Executive Secretary, Division of College Work of the Protestant Episcopal Church, New York, N. Y. (30)